BON SCOTT
HAVE A DRINK ON ME

Have a Drink on Me

Irene Thornton

with Simone Ubaldi

For Eric

BON SCOTT

A catalogue record for this book is available from the British Library

This edition © Red Planet Publishing Ltd 2017. Text © Red Planet Publishing Ltd 2018
Reprinted 2019

ISBN: 978 1 9113 4670 8

Printed in the UK

Page design / layout / cover: Harry Gregory
Publisher: Mark Neeter

Red Planet Publishing Ltd,
Tremough Innovation Centre,
Penryn, Cornwall TR10 9TA

www.redplanetzone.com
Email: info@redplanetzone.com

⚡ HAVE A DRINK ON ME ⚡

PROLOGUE

I met a prominent South Australian politician a few years ago. At least, I tried to meet him. He was a friend of my friend Andrea, an independent senator who fought for ordinary working people, and I really admired him. *I'm going to shake his hand,* I thought. It took a bit of nerve because I'm not the most confident person, particularly in crowds.

We were at Andrea's 60th birthday party at her home in Adelaide, surrounded by party guests, and half of them had the same idea as me. I needed an introduction but Andrea wasn't around, so I hovered nearby with a drink in my hand, looking like a spare part. *Nice to meet you,* I rehearsed in my head, *I just wanted to say...*

While I hovered, I pretended I was engrossed in a photograph on Andrea's wall. It was a picture of me, taken forty years earlier, photocopied and attached limply with a single piece of Blu-Tack. It was a photo of my ex and I on our wedding day, two young kids in funny Seventies clothing. I'd seen it a thousand times before. Anyway, I wasn't really paying attention to the picture. I was listening to the senator and waiting for an opportunity to introduce myself, hoping desperately that I didn't look like I was just standing there, waiting for an opportunity to introduce myself.

I was about to give up on the whole thing when the person the politician had been talking to excused themself. *Right,* I thought, *here goes.* I reached out my hand and the word 'hello' was just forming in my mouth when a young guy leapt in between us. The politician was a bit startled because the young man was very pissed, very excited, and talking *very loudly*.

'Hey tell me something!' he said to me, eyes wide. 'That's you, isn't it? That's you!'

He was pointing at the picture on the wall.

'Yeah, long time ago,' I mumbled.

'And that's...?' he shouted, pointing at my ex.

I laughed at him and shook my head in embarrassment, colour creeping into my cheeks. The kid was nearly beside himself. The politician was looking at the photo with a confused expression on his face.

'Go on, say it!' the guy pressed. 'Say it, go on!'

I sighed and smiled.

'That's Bon Scott,' I replied.

'Bon Scott!' the kid shouted, then turned to the senator to yell drunkenly in his face. 'She was married to Bon Scott!'

The young guy was over the moon but I was mortified. I gave the politician a weak smile, but he still looked confused. I didn't get to shake his hand, because the kid had a lot of questions and he wasn't going to let me go until I answered all of them, every single one.

It wasn't the first time something like that had happened to me, but it was always strange when it did. I told a friend about it later and she was delighted.

'You know, there are more people in the world that know about Bon than about your beloved senator,' she laughed.

'Sure, but I'm not Bon. I'm Bon Scott's wife. Or I was Bon Scott's wife, forty years ago.'

'The kid was just jogging your memory,' she said.

I laughed at her and shook my head.

As if I could ever forget.

PART ONE

JUST IRENE

⚡

There are two-thousand kilometres between Adelaide and Perth, but I don't think much else separates them. Bon Scott grew up in the suburbs of a hot, remote Australian city surrounded by long, white beaches. My suburbs were very similar to his. As Australian kids growing up in the Fifties and Sixties, we were isolated from the rest of the world. It was beamed in on our black-and-white television sets; we heard about it on the radio and in the cinema, but it was still very far away. The real world didn't extend much beyond your front door, not back then. The real world was dry lawns, Hills Hoists and a roast dinner on Sundays.

I was born in Port Pirie in 1950, a country town on the South Australian coast about two hours' drive from Adelaide. It was a dusty place - home to a smelting plant, a gritty shell beach and a few faded weatherboard houses. My parents were Port Pirie people, born and bred; simple, honest, and in my Dad's case, slightly down in the mouth.

'If I've got enough money, would you like to go out to the pictures on Saturday?' he asked Mum.

She said yes as an act of kindness. Later, she told me she had always liked men with dark, curly hair. Dad was blonde, but he convinced her to marry him anyway. He was a good man.

Mum had worked in her parents' corner store but she gave that up to be a housewife while Dad went to work as a draftsman. They had a son, my older brother Peter, when Dad went off to fight in the war. When he came home again, a bit worse for wear, he and Mum had three more kids - my sister Kathleen, my sister Fay, and me. Kathleen was the eldest girl, I was the middle child with sunny blonde hair, and Fay was the baby. I called Fay my little blister (instead of my sister) because she was always tagging along behind me, driving me nuts.

Port Pirie was too small for a growing family so Dad cast his line a bit farther afield and snagged a job in Adelaide. When I was four or five, we moved to the big city - or the bigger city, at least. Adelaide was impressive compared to Port Pirie, but it was no gleaming metropolis. Even when the population climbed over a million, people still called it Australia's largest country town. To me, it felt like one endless suburb; picket fence after picket fence, as far as the eye could see.

My family lived in a red-brick Californian bungalow, with a long, shady porch out front. There were two bedrooms and a third makeshift room towards the back of the house, which was closed off with a curtain hanging from a piece of string. We were sardined into the place, but it was generally pretty comfortable, except in summer. When it was too hot, we slept on the floor in the hallway or on a blanket out on the front lawn. We weren't very well off, but I wasn't aware of it at the time. My life seemed pretty ordinary.

I remember what most Australians remember about their childhood; running under the sprinkler in the baking January heat, heading off on long adventures on my bike. I was a happy little kid, with bangs and pigtails and nice clothes to wear to church on Sundays. I played tennis and netball, and I really loved to read, mostly English adventure novels and Archie comics. I was a bit of a dreamer. *Irene spends too much time staring out of the window*, my school reports read, *but she is very polite and courteous*. I was good at English but terrible at arithmetic, no matter how much help my father gave me with homework.

After school, I skipped rope and played in the vacant church tennis courts with other kids from the neighbourhood, drew on the footpath in chalk and raced paper boats down storm drains. On the weekends, or when I was lucky enough to have a day off school, Mum took me to the matinee session at the local movie theatre. I had stars in my eyes, the way little girls do. I collected old magazines with black-and-white pictures of Hollywood legends, like Jean Harlow, Audrey Hepburn and Clark Gable. They were no different to me than the characters in fairy tales.

When you live in a small world, people take their cues from their neighbours, not reality TV. If my father painted the house, the house up the road would be painted a week later, and people noticed if you didn't mow the lawn regularly. On the other hand, we actually spent time with our neighbours. They were our closest friends. On Friday nights, my whole family would climb through a hole in the fence to watch television with the lady next door, and half the time the kids would fall asleep on the lino under the table, or propped up against the couch, while the adults drank beer and ate biscuits and talked. It wasn't particularly exciting but it was the only life we knew.

My Dad passed away when I was ten, sadly. My brother Peter had moved back to Port Pirie to study metallurgy and work at the smelting plant, so Mum was left with three girls to raise on a war widow's pension. My father's death was a shock and it made me quite introverted, and being introverted in my early teens made me a bit uncertain socially. I became quite a nervous person, and second-guessed myself a lot, but it all happened inside my head. On the surface, I stuck my chin out and had a serious independent streak.

Our family struggled, but we got by. It took Mum a long while to get over Dad's death and even longer to get her sense of humour back, but she focused on her kids and found a way to carry on. Dinner was always on the table at six (the vegetables had usually been boiling since three) and our clothes were always clean and ironed. Mum was very simple and very good, though she loved a bit of slapstick. She sat in bed every night eating an apple and reading the bible, but good luck if you bumped your head on a kitchen cupboard; Mum would be too busy laughing to bandage you up.

Kathleen was quite glamorous as a teenager, honey blonde and attractive with big bones and big curves, and plenty of interest from the boys. She was the polar opposite of me. I was a waif, standing off to one side of the schoolyard, lost in my thoughts. The one thing we had in common was art. Kathleen was a very talented illustrator, and when I was still young she let me tag along to her Saturday art classes at a nearby technical college. I loved to draw - I got the gift from my Dad, who did amazing illustrations. I wasn't particularly good at painting but I drew really excellent cartoons, and once I'd gotten into the habit of doing them I never stopped. Throughout my life, whenever someone bothered me or made me laugh with a particular quirk, I drew a caricature of them. It's a good feeling when you know you've captured someone perfectly, especially if they have a really unique character. I drew a lot of pictures of Bon over the years.

I loved music, even as a kid. The radio was always on at home and I feel like I always had a song in my head, tunes from the Forties and Fifties that my mother adored. The old songs still come back to me - Jim Reeves and Kitty Lester, 'But I Do' by Clarence

'Frogman' Henry and 'A White Sport Coat (And a Pink Carnation)' by Marty Robbins. I'll start humming them to myself over the dishes, half a century later.

But my life really changed when I heard The Beatles. 'Love Me Do' came out when I was twelve and I adored it. They had such a radically different sound, with such beautiful harmonies, that a line was drawn between them and everything that had come before. The Beatles were the first musicians I really knew and loved, and the first band that belonged to me instead of my Mum. When they came to Adelaide in 1964, I went into the city to see them. I was too young to go to the concert, but I took a bus into town and stood in a sea of screaming kids while the Fab Four came out and waved at us from the hotel balcony, little specks in the distance. It's hard to explain how strange the experience was. The world of Elvis and The Beatles and British rock was a million miles away from my front lawn, but suddenly they were right there, in Adelaide. It was the first time I felt like that distant world had a real three-dimensional shape - if I could just get close enough, I could actually reach out and touch them. Add to that the screaming hysteria of a few thousand young fans and you can imagine the impression the experience made on my tiny little brain.

I saw my first live band about a year later at the scout hall around the corner from my house. They were called The Silhouettes and they played Beatles covers, plus songs by The Animals and The Troggs, and other great bands of that era. The sheer volume of it really blew my mind; they must have been playing on crappy little PA systems, but the music was still louder than I'd ever heard it before. People were dancing, too, which was just incredible. It was like stepping on to a different planet.

A lot of kids went out to see bands play in the Sixties, so I was hardly unusual, but I was probably a bit more dedicated than your average teen. Shows were advertised on posters and on the radio, and I'd catch buses to go and see them, trekking out to the suburbs or into the city. It was an amazing time for music in Adelaide; there were clubs, halls and venues all over the place and some of the biggest Australian bands of the era were based in my hometown. Glenn Shorrock played in The Twilights and they were huge; I saw them play all the time. The Masters Apprentices was another local act, although they called themselves The Mustangs and played surf-rock tunes by The Shadows back then. I used to watch them perform in coffee lounges, which were shitty little places that sold toasted sandwiches, fruit juice and what must have been the world's worst coffee.

When I got older I saw bands play in pubs, but in the early days it was all very innocent. Sober teenagers filed into the hall, danced, clapped politely and left. But I thought it was really cool. I was impressed with how the people at gigs dressed; they seemed far more fashionable than the kids at school. The girls wore miniskirts and the boys wore button-up shirts and stovepipe pants, and turtlenecks when they came in style. I loved clothes almost as much as I loved music and I enjoyed dressing up to go out, in outfits stitched together on Mum's old sewing machine. As I got older, I added a ton of black eye make-up and red lipstick, which ended up smeared all over Mum's towels at the end of the night. My poor, long-suffering mother never complained, and she didn't bat an eye no matter how short my skirts got.

'You look lovely dear,' she'd say meekly. 'Just don't swear because it spoils the way you look.'

My fashion sense, like the music I loved, was imported from overseas. There were loads of great Australian bands but hardly any of them were playing original music - the guys who picked up guitars in the mid-Sixties were still trying to imitate their idols; they hadn't even considered competing with them. Australia was just an outpost for the British music scene, connected to Mother England via the 'Ten Pound Poms'. In Adelaide especially, which had a huge expat community in the outer suburb of Elizabeth, English-Australian kids with relatives back home brought the latest fashion and music from the UK and transplanted it in our backyards.

I'd see them riding the long, flat Adelaide roads on motorised scooters, in their three-piece suits and anoraks, looking totally out of place. In England, they would have been called Mods. They had a huge influence on Australian rock 'n' roll.

Bon Scott's family was Scottish, but they came to Australia with the rest of the Ten Pound Poms as part of an assisted passage scheme to encourage British migration to Australia in the post-war years. Their tickets cost ten pounds apiece, which was a very cheap way into the lucky country. A land of sunshine and opportunity was waiting for anyone with the tenner in their pocket; it just happened to be at the arse-end of the universe.

Bon was six when the Scott family migrated, landing in Melbourne before resettling in Perth. Chick had moved them for much the same reason my Dad moved us - he was restless after the war. Australia had a booming economy and land to spare, including plenty of land where the Scott boys could run wild. There was Bon (born Ronald Belford Scott on July 9, 1946), his brother Derek (three years younger) and Graeme (born in Melbourne circa 1953), and the three of them needed a lot of room to grow.

The family settled in Fremantle, an old port at the mouth of the Swan River, and Bon and his brothers became little fish, disappearing to the river whenever they could, launching themselves off old tree branches and stuffing around in the water. They rode their bikes, played sports and read comic books; they made friends with kids in the neighbourhood, got into scrapes and found ways to entertain themselves without video games or smartphones. When it was hot, they went to the beach. When they were bored, they went looking for adventure. Bon was a very social kid, according to Isa, and she often had to drag him away from friends just to get him to the house for dinner.

Like me, Bon didn't excel at school, although he probably didn't try as hard as I did. From when he was a toddler, marching through the streets of Kirriemuir with the local pipe band, his mission in life was clear. He was going to be a musician. He played the drums on whatever he could find, whether it was Isa's pots or the breadbox. He wanted to learn piano, but he wouldn't go to the lessons. Then Chick bought him an accordion and Bon gave that a try (it wasn't nearly loud enough). His parents finally relented and traded the accordion for a drum kit, and all of a sudden Bon's talent took off. He joined the Scots club pipe band in Fremantle and played the drums alongside his father, and became a novice champion in

14

drumming at the tender age of twelve. He wore a kilt and played traditional Scottish music right up until he turned seventeen.

Bon was a few years older than me. He fell in love with rock 'n' roll in the late Fifties, with Elvis, Jerry Lee Lewis and Chuck Berry. The image of the rock 'n' roll rebel stuck with him, and it went hand-in-hand with his own teenage antics. Bon was a working class kid in a rough port town; he started to smoke, he roamed in a gang and he learned how to fight. He dropped out of school when he was fifteen and spent nine months in a boys' prison when he was sixteen (for stealing petrol and some other minor offences). When he got out of prison, Bon got some tattoos. He was a tough young man by then. He didn't play in a rock 'n' roll band until he was almost nineteen, but he was already living a rock 'n' roll life.

The 'British Invasion' was well and truly underway when Bon joined his first band, a covers act called The Spektors. Like everyone else, they were dazzled by The Beatles and then floored by The Rolling Stones, and they did their best to imitate their heroes, but they were a teenybopper band. They played crowd-pleasing, unsophisticated music and tried their best to look cute. And that was enough. In the year that they were together, The Spektors built a decent following on the Perth dance-hall circuit. Then in 1966, they merged with their local rivals, The Winstons, to become The Valentines. Bon took co-lead-singer duties with The Winstons' singer, Vince Lovegrove, and together they decided to become professional musicians. The Valentines were ambitious, inspired by the success of The Twilights and The Masters Apprentices, as well as Billy Thorpe and The Aztecs and The Easybeats out of Sydney. They released their first single in 1967, and made the number five spot on the local chart. Shortly afterwards, they left Perth for Melbourne, to try their luck at being real pop stars.

I saw The Valentines on television, although I never saw them live. There were shows like Kommotion and The Go!! Show in the Sixties, which had bands on to perform their latest hit single. The Valentines were on a show called Uptight to mime along to 'Build Me Up, Buttercup', wearing puffy-sleeve shirts and these terrible satin pants. I thought Bon was really cute, but the band was really awful. I'd seen enough good music by then to know crap when I heard it.

I did my own exploring and record-collecting, but I also had a couple of boyfriends who introduced me to some really great stuff. I met the first guy at the same scout hall where I saw my first gig. His name was Phillip and he stood out like the proverbials because he had long hair (meaning hair that grew very slightly past his ears). He looked really different and exciting to me. I was very taken with him. Phillip said he was tossing up between me and a girlfriend of mine that lived down the road, but he chose me in the end. (He probably flipped a coin.) We danced together and I think he bought me some punch, and I ended up dating him for a couple of years. It was all very innocent. We went to see bands together and would neck in the corner at the end of the night, but it never went any further than that. I actually dropped him a couple of times but he kept coming back. He turned up at Mum's in a new sports car one evening and she convinced me to patch it up and go for a drive with him, which I reluctantly agreed to do. I dropped him again afterwards because he was a terrible driver.

By that stage, I had left school and joined the workforce. I went to business college when I was sixteen to learn typing and shorthand, then found myself a job at a family-owned white goods store. (The boss came round to meet my mother and assure her they'd take good care of me.) The best thing about working was that I suddenly had my own money. I could buy records, make-up and beer whenever I wanted, and pay for taxis to get home at the end of the night. Being financially independent meant a lot to me. I left the white goods store after six months and I went to work in a lawyer's office, typing up the dictation on old carbon copy paper, but I didn't last long. I kept handing in typed documents full of gaps because I couldn't read my own shorthand. Unsurprisingly, they sacked me. My next stop was the public service, at the Department of Motor Vehicles, typing and filing car registrations. I must have lifted my game at that point because I held on to that job for a while.

I met a lot of people at work that I wouldn't normally spend time with, and got used to the idea that that's what life is about - you spend most of your time clocking on and clocking off, pretending to be interested in your workmates' conversation. Some of them were nice. I became quite good friends with a girl called Andrea, who went op-shopping with me before op-shopping was in fashion and loved to draw nearly as much as I did. Andrea was a very capable, industrious kind of person; I'd go around to her house and find her up on the roof banging away at something or out the back, making a pair of shoes. She also had a horse. I found her up at the stables one day with a snake wrapped around her waist.

'Do you like my live belt?' she grinned.

Andrea was about six foot tall but she had a very breathless, girlish way of talking. She was very beautiful, I thought, with her lovely olive skin. She became my closest friend, although we had very different personalities. I was in awe of her. I was very sensitive and Andrea was very practical. She was confident, whereas I felt awkward in social situations a lot of the time. The truth is, I had pretty low self-esteem, which is how I ended up dating 'The Bastard'.

When I was seventeen, my social life revolved around music. There were daytime and afternoon gigs and lots of shows in the evening, and the evening shows rolled into other things. You'd jump in the car and head off to a party for more drinking, more talk and more music, and inevitably you'd meet people who liked the same stuff as you. I met the bastard at one of these parties. He was sitting in a corner with his mates, making sarcastic comments about the other party guests. I thought he looked really arty and different; he was wearing a strange quilted jacket that he'd pilfered from the costume department of Fiddler on the Roof, and his face was really angular and handsome. He was incredibly confident - he fancied himself quite the intellectual. I think I was naïve enough to be impressed.

The Bastard started chatting to me at the party and eventually came around to asking me out, but I'm not entirely sure why. We began dating, but he was never that enthusiastic about the relationship, a point he demonstrated repeatedly the whole time it was going on. I had no phone at Mum's so I had to wait around for him to come and see me; sometimes he turned up and sometimes he didn't. When he did come over, he was awkward as hell and clearly would have preferred to be somewhere else.

'Your mother's bathroom must be the only one in the world where you come out dirtier than when you went in,' he once said.

I got properly drunk for the first time in The Bastard's company and it was a pretty miserable experience. We were out at the pub with a group of his friends when he handed me a bottle of scotch.

'See if you can drink it down to here,' he grinned.

I didn't want to lose face in front of the boys so I knocked it back, as instructed, and shortly afterwards was completely legless. The Bastard drove me home, rang the doorbell and took off as soon as my mother answered. Later, he introduced me to drugs. We took these things called Purple Hearts when I was drunk enough not to think twice about it, then The Bastard disappeared. I ended up sitting in a car with Andrea and her boyfriend out front of Mum's place in the early hours of the morning, chatting away until the morning milk was delivered. (Andrea got thirsty and stole a bottle of milk off the neighbour's veranda.)

Obviously I shouldn't have liked The Bastard, but I did. He seemed to know a lot about everything, particularly art. He got me reading novels and took me to the South Australian Film Festival, and he signed me up to the Australian Record Club so I could keep on top of all the amazing music that was coming out of England.

It was the late Sixties and the music scene had well and truly changed by then. Everyone was obsessed with Led Zeppelin, Deep Purple and The Beatles' White Album. That psychedelic rock sound hadn't trickled down to the live music scene yet, but it was all you heard at parties. The Bastard was a big fan. I sat meekly next to him when we went out and watched him and his friends get stoned and talk endless hours of shit about the new sound coming out of the UK. I thought his opinions were incredibly clever and interesting. I think I idolised him, which is far more than he deserved. It kept the relationship going for a couple of years, which was a couple of years longer than it should have kept going. He had great taste, he just wasn't very nice.

The Bastard was the last guy I dated before Bon. I hate to even mention him, but the person I was when I met Bon Scott was deeply influenced by my relationship with the world's shittiest boyfriend, in good ways and bad. On the one hand, he made me very guarded and fragile, and determined not to look stupid. On the other hand, The Bastard helped me to become quite headstrong and self-reliant. He brought me to England, though he didn't actually want me to be there.

In late 1969, when I was about nineteen, my shitty boyfriend went off to Singapore for a holiday, or at least that's what he told me he was doing. He had actually moved to London, but he went to the trouble of writing fake letters and having his student friends in Singapore post them to me on his behalf. The Bastard's father was outraged and let the truth slip when I went around to visit one day. I was angry and I was mortified. Unfortunately, I was also really heartbroken because I'd managed to convince myself that I was in love with the guy. (As a side note, this didn't stop me from having a revenge fling with one of The Bastard's very respected acquaintances.)

The Bastard felt pretty awful for lying and getting caught, and he asked me to join him in London. And because I was a terrible idiot, I decided to go. I sold practically everything I had to pay for the flight, including the typewriter Mum had bought me.

'Go and get it back!' she cried. 'I gave up smoking to pay for that thing.'

I had barely left Adelaide since I moved there as a child and London might as well have been the Moon. I didn't hesitate or ask for permission, mind you; I didn't actually tell

Mum I was going until after the ticket was booked. I thought of myself as quite a nervous and timid thing, but when it came down to it I was perfectly cool. I turned up at the airport with a miniskirt and a new set of luggage and boarded the flight without looking back. Mum was awe-struck.

She said, 'You got on that plane like you'd done it a hundred times before.'

I didn't know what to be afraid of. I had no idea about other countries and cultures. We had a stopover in Bahrain, and there I was in the miniskirt surrounded by Arabic men holding machine guns. It wouldn't have occurred to me in a million years that my outfit wasn't appropriate. I just thought it was fantastic, like being in a film.

London was an even bigger thrill. It was the tail end of the 'Swinging Sixties' and I missed the whole Carnaby Street scene by a couple of years, but it was still an electrifying place to be. There were fascinating people everywhere you looked, not just the odd, slightly unusual person who popped up in Adelaide. I loved the whole English pub scene, with open fires and winter light coming through the stained-glass windows. I loved the markets on the Kensington high street, which were full of handicrafts and things that you'd never find in the shops. I loved the feeling of being self-sufficient, figuring out how to read the tube map and get myself around that massive city. I felt like I was part of something, without even having to try.

I worked as a live-in maid for a wealthy couple in Chelsea, burning rissoles and bumping their vacuum cleaner as I dragged it up and down the stairs. My flat was in the basement of their house and the windows were below street level. It was like climbing out of the earth every time I walked up the stairs, and I felt this dread that I would never reach the open air. Adelaide was flat and wide and spacious, but London hunched over you. Everything was grey; the footpaths, the buildings, the sky. But it was exciting, too. I didn't realise it until I left, but I was bored with the blandness and backwardness of Adelaide. London felt like the centre of the world.

The Bastard had a job at an art gallery, so he took me to the occasional art exhibition and to screenings at the British Film Institute. Mick Jagger's 'Performance' opened while we were in town and he got us tickets, and I saw more live music than I can remember. There were tons of gigs in Camden Town and in Soho bars, south of Oxford Street; Rod Stewart played with The Faces in a venue that was basically a big school hall.

As the year rolled on, we took trips around Britain, to Hampton Court Castle and Stratford-upon-Avon, then north up to Scotland to a place called Galashiels. In the summer, we went to Amsterdam and visited Anne Frank's house, and I learned that there are places in the world where people have slabs of cold meat and cheese for breakfast instead of Weetabix. On another weekend, we hitched to Dover and met a young French lawyer on the ferry to Calais. He drove us into Paris in his convertible and put us up in his apartment on Rue Bayen, then ferried us from the Eiffel Tower and the Arc de Triomphe to all these fantastic clubs and restaurants.

When we travelled together, The Bastard and I had a lot of fun, but there were times in London when I hardly felt like I even had a boyfriend. He lived with his mates in a dingy flat in West London, and spent most of his time with his head in a cloud of dope, listening to records and talking crap. People smoked and talked crap at parties back in Adelaide, but it was a laugh. In London, he'd get stoned and have a four-hour conversation about a guitar solo. It was incredibly tedious.

He rarely made plans with me, and when he did he often wouldn't turn up, or he'd make plans with other people and make it clear he didn't want me tagging along. I would arrive somewhere to meet him, only to discover that he'd already left, and turn around to catch two tube trains home with my tail between my legs. Of course it seems obvious now that he wasn't very interested in me, but he didn't want me seeing anyone else either. I met a lot of lovely guys in London, funnily enough, but The Bastard had a habit of showing up at just the wrong moment and treating me like his property.

As the year dragged on, I got tired of him. I left my job as a maid and went to work as a typist at Australia House, and moved in with a fantastic group of girls who were all my own age. We played loud music and danced around the flat, and went out to pubs and parties together. The longer I stayed in London, the less I saw of my boyfriend, and the less I really cared. Christmas rolled around and he was nowhere to be seen, but I was happier than I had been in a long while. It snowed on Christmas Day. I was in the flat with the girls trying to cook a turkey when these little flakes came drifting down past the window, and I was so excited I ran out into the street. There were people standing around outside the local pub, singing Christmas carols and drinking beer and watching it snow. I waved at them with a big, silly grin on my face. It was absolutely magic.

I decided to go home in the new year. There was no drama at all, no big announcement. I just told The Bastard I was leaving, and he shrugged to let me know that he didn't really care. I realised in that moment how unpleasant he was, how mean and mocking and sarcastic he had always been towards me - although in fairness he was like that with a lot of people. Whatever love I thought I had for him was beaten out of me with snide comments and cruel behaviour. I was more than ready to walk away.

I was ashamed that I'd followed a guy who didn't love me half way around the world, but I didn't regret going to London. It was a huge eye-opener for me. I had been to those magic, far-off places and seen them with my own eyes, which was a rare experience back in those days. I didn't think it made me any more interesting, but I felt like I was my own person. If nothing else, I knew I could take care of myself. And I would take care of myself, especially when it came to men. I wouldn't let anyone take me for a fool, even though I felt foolish. I had all the pride in the world, but absolutely no confidence.

PART TWO

MRS BON SCOTT

⚡

CHAPTER 1

I desperately wanted to be back in Adelaide right up until I got there. I spent a lot of time feeling homesick in London, and then I wondered why the hell I ever left. Adelaide was such a culture shock. There was no tube to the front door, Mum's place didn't have a phone. But it was more than that, really. The city felt wrong. It hardly felt like a city at all.

I got a job as a shorthand typist a few days after I arrived, at an air-conditioning company near the railway yards. It was a dustbowl next to a highway in the middle of shitsville; the only sign of life was the trucks rattling past the window. I had all the open sky I wanted but nothing else, just the endless, flat roads of Australia's biggest country town. Kathleen was married and living with her husband, but my little sister Fay was still at home, although neither of us had a car. I had to wait for my friends to drop around and pick me up, or I relied on public transport. The stinking hot buses and overground trains were miserable, but my independent streak was as wide as a house. I wouldn't let anything stop me from living my life. I remember hopping off the train one day, in a little lime-coloured dress and my skinny, tanned legs, and walking straight into the front bar of the Reepham Hotel on the corner of Regency Road. It was quite a rough place, but I was undaunted. I stood at the bar and ordered a schooner of beer, downed it in one gulp and turned to walk out again.

'Night, Bill,' a barman called after me, and the locals all broke down laughing.

Andrea came to visit me the night I got back from England, when I was still sagging from the trip.

'You seem like a really old lady,' she said. I was so jet-lagged I could barely roll my eyes at her.

Andrea had come over with our friend Julie, in a car they had borrowed from Julie's new boyfriend, a guy named Vince Lovegrove. Julie had taken up with Vince while I was in London and they were living together by the time I came home.

A few days later, I went round to visit Andrea and she told me about the people she'd met while I was away, musicians she had met through Julie and Vince. She wanted to take me to this place in the Adelaide Hills, a farm on the fringe of the city that had become quite a happening scene. There was a band living up there called Fraternity and they threw the best parties, Andrea said. She wanted to introduce me to the singer. It was obvious that Andrea had a bit of a crush on this bloke. She had a dreamy way of speaking about him that gave her away. She told me that she had been wrestling with the guy, just messing around, but he was every bit as strong as her. I knew this was a big deal for Andrea; she was such a mountain that most men seemed puny in comparison.

We headed off to the hills the following weekend, to a place called Hemming's Farm in Aldgate, a sprawling property on three-and-a-half acres out on Cricklewood Road. It was a single-storey building, modern for the time, with glass walls out the back and a long stretch of grass that dipped down towards a marshy pool of water - a little country dam. Andrea told me the house belonged to a guy called Hamish Henry and that Hamish was Fraternity's manager.

'He's not *well off*,' she giggled, 'He's *very, very rich.*'

Hamish had a day job at the family business, State City Motors, but his passion was music. He had coaxed Fraternity from Sydney to Adelaide in January 1971, just a few months before I got home, and together they were going to take over the world. Until that happened, Hamish was going to pay the bills. He shipped the entire band over to South Australia and put them up at Hemming's Farm, and the farm became the centre of a cool little scene. Adelaide was dead in the early Seventies, far more so than even five years earlier. When I was a teenager, there were house parties every weekend, gigs and parties at Adelaide University, and a big crowd of music fans that moved from pub to pub, but Hemming's Farm was out on its own in 1971. They had three-day benders out there, fuelled by dope and mushrooms and speed and booze. Fraternity played in town several nights a week and the crowd would follow them back after the show, picking up strays like Andrea along the way.

Andrea wasn't really into music, but she liked a party as much as anyone else.

As time went on, a lot of people starting referring to Fraternity as a kind of hippy act and Hemming's Farm as a commune, but it was pure rock 'n' roll up there. The guys wore RM Williams boots and shirts, and they were right into Bob Dylan and The Band. It was more country-rock than anything else. It didn't feel like a hippy place at all. It was packed when Andrea and I arrived, with people spilling out of doors and music blaring through the windows. There were pockets of action everywhere; people standing around having a laugh, moving through the rooms, sitting around on the grass outside. I felt anxious as I climbed out of the car because there were so many strange faces, but I pushed my chin out and pushed the feeling away. It was odd, realising that life in Adelaide had just continued on without me.

The sun was beating down and I felt overdressed in my frilly dress and black suede boots, but I'm sure nobody noticed; everywhere you looked, people were busy getting pissed and stoned. It seemed like the sort of party that would be a lot of fun if you were with your friends, though I was a bit of a spare part. Andrea drifted off and I settled down inside to watch people milling about. At some point I realised Doug Parkinson was sitting next to me, which was a bit bizarre. He was a singer, very well known back then. He struck up a conversation with me and I think he wanted to chat me up, but he didn't get anywhere. I was happy to sit and observe the crowd. It felt like half of Adelaide was on that farm, a wide mix of young people and older, arty types, all thrown in together, all having a laugh.

Andrea had reappeared and taken a seat next to me just as a commotion broke out on the other side of the room.
She grinned and pointed, 'There he is.'

This was the bloke she'd been on about, this macho-man wrestler, the lead singer of Fraternity. *Jesus*, I thought. The guy who came stumbling through the crowd was wearing nothing but a spray-on pair of tiny denim shorts. He had a girl in one arm and a drink in the other, and he was stumbling left and right through the throng of people as he laughed his head off. He was a wiry-looking thing, much shorter than Andrea.

'His name is Bon Scott,' she said.

I didn't think much of him.

I had a great time at the party, in the end. A few drinks in, I felt quite at home, not that I had a clue where anything was. I went searching for the toilet at one point, opening every door I came across to empty rooms and dead ends, right up until the very last door. I opened it and froze in my tracks. Bon was naked in front of me, kneeling on the end of the bed with a girl's foot in his mouth. He turned around and gave me a surprised look with his lips still wrapped around a couple of her toes.

'Sorry,' I stammered. 'I didn't mean to interrupt.'

I closed the door, surprised and disgusted. I hadn't heard of toe-sucking before and I found the whole scene pretty alarming. It was so much worse than if I'd stumbled in on them doing it; I couldn't get the image of that girl's foot out of my head.

The next time I saw Bon he had more clothes on. Julie was working in a shop in Rundle Mall, in the middle of the city, and I popped in one day to say hello. We were having a chat at the counter with another couple of girls when we were startled by a series of loud thumps, barrelling down towards us. The shop was in a basement and Bon had decided to make a grand entrance by somersaulting down the stairs. We thought it was an accident at first and all four of us gasped in shock, but Bon bounced to his feet and started laughing, and the other girls joined in. I might have smiled a little bit, but mostly I just rolled my eyes. Julie introduced us to each other and Bon said hello, but I didn't rate a second glance after that. He chatted with Julie and the other girls, and as quick as he came he was off again, bouncing back up the stairs. I didn't know what to make of him. He was a ball of energy and clearly a bit mad. I couldn't quite see what Andrea was on about, but he was certainly a scene-stealer. I don't think I'd met anyone like that before. I wasn't sure I liked Bon, but I couldn't help but notice him. He'd virtually break his neck to get your attention.

I found out later that Julie had been talking me up to him, plotting to get the two of us together.

'You wait 'til you meet my friend, Irene,' she told him.

I don't know what he thought of me that day. If he noticed me, he did his best to hide it.

It can't have been more than a couple of weeks later that I saw Fraternity play live. Vince took me along to a gig at the Largs Pier Hotel, which was notorious in those days. It's legendary now. It was just a pub, really, but half the Australian rock stars of the 1970s played there, before they were famous or on the way up.

Vince Lovegrove was a music journalist and also ran a booking agency. He had been part of the Australian music scene since the Sixties, when he'd got his start playing in bubblegum pop groups. He and Bon went way back, all the way back to Perth. They formed The Valentines together; two swinging lead singers in Australia's worst teenybopper band. The Valentines had had a decent run in the late Sixties and developed a reasonable fan base, but their fans were all dizzy young girls. In 1969, they supported The Easybeats and wrote songs with Harry Vanda and George Young. They made several television appearances and had a couple of minor hits, including a tune called 'My Old Man's a Groovy Old Man' and bizarre cover of 'Nick Nack Paddy Wack' that never should have happened. The Valentines toured relentlessly for a couple of years but they just weren't very good, and after a failed attempt at reinventing themselves in a psychedelic mould, they decided to break up. Vince and Bon just grew out of it, I think, and they both moved on to other things. Coincidentally, they both ended up in Adelaide.

I had only just met Vince but I liked him a lot. He had a really quick wit. He was writing for Go-Set, the Australian music bible, and had his own music television show in Adelaide called Move. Vince really dug Bon's new band, but then plenty of people did. In early 1970, Fraternity was supposed to be Australia's next big thing. They were playing mostly original material, which was still pretty unusual, and they had just finished a tour supporting Jerry Lee Lewis. The local music industry was raving about them, but I didn't know a thing about it. No one was talking about Austra- lian bands in London.

I had also never been to the Largs Pier Hotel. It was on the beach, just past Semaphore in the seaside suburb of Largs. The pub sat on a corner block - three stories high, with big, old, arched windows from top to bottom - and every inch of the place was full. When Vince and I rocked up, it was heaving. It was the middle of summer and people were coming straight off the beach and up to the pub, spilling out over the footpath in their towels and togs. It was an unbelievable piss-up; hundreds of people, all drinking and dancing, all having a bloody good time. It had the most amazing atmosphere.

Fraternity were on stage when we arrived and they were loud. The sound hit you like a wall the second you walked inside, a big bluesy rock 'n' roll sound with a progressive country feel. There was a sea of people in the room and all eyes were fixed on Bon. And to my surprise, he was quite something to look at. For a compact sort of bloke, he really commanded your attention. His voice was powerful, but it was the way he moved that drew you in. It was incredibly slick and theatrical. He swung his hips, spun around on the spot and leaned right back into the notes. I'd never seen anything like it. When he danced, his arms were slightly outstretched, elbows bending in time with the music. Much later, I discovered that he had named his own dance moves.

'Look,' he smiled at a gig one night, 'They're all doing it!'

'Doing what?' I asked.

'The *Bon*.'

That first night at the Largs Pier, I started to understand Bon's appeal. I don't know if I was impressed exactly, but the band sounded great and Bon was just something else. I found it quite hard to look away. During the break between sets, he came over to say hello and Vince introduced me yet again.

'Hello,' Bon grinned.

He was wearing the tightest pair of jeans I had ever seen; they didn't leave much to the imagination. Sometimes things blurt out of my mouth before my brain has a chance to kick in and that night was one of the classics.

I looked down at his crotch and said, 'What a well-packed lunch.'

'Yeah,' he winked. 'Two boiled eggs and a sausage.'

He didn't miss a beat and it made me laugh out loud. *Hello*, I thought. I was suddenly *very* impressed.

Most of the guys in Fraternity were living up in the hills when I met Bon, but he was living in town with Bruce Howe (the bass player), John Bisset (the keyboardist), John's wife Cheryl and their four-year-old kid. Their house at 67 Norwood Parade was a complete contrast to Hemming's Farm. It was an old sandstone Federation building with a beautiful veranda out the front and a huge back yard, smack bang in the middle of things. There was a milk bar on the corner, a big shopping strip up the road and a chicken shop next door; Bon used to climb out of the bedroom window to buy his dinner, then climb back in and eat roast chicken in bed.

Hamish paid the rent on the Norwood place as well as the farm, though I'm not really sure why the band needed two houses. I think John and Cheryl wanted a bit of privacy and Bon wanted to be closer to the pub. He was closer to his friends, as well. Bon spent a lot of time over at Vince and Julie's place in North Adelaide (a house they rented from Hamish - it was all a bit incestuous). Bon had a temporary little room set up at Vince's place, too; an old pantry space just off the kitchen that was just big enough to fit a bed. Don't ask me why he needed two rooms.

I went around to visit Julie one day, just after that night at the Largs Pier, and found Bon in the middle of the lounge room ironing the creases out of a pair of jeans. It should have been awkward, but I was distracted by what he was doing. *Who irons jeans?* I thought. He was an incredibly fussy person when it came to his clothes, a real neat freak, and he wasn't at all embarrassed about it.

A mutual friend told me later that Bon had mentioned me early on.

'I've met this real spunk,' he said, 'But she doesn't want to know about me.'

I felt the same way after that night at the Largs Pier, but I didn't let on when I saw him again. I think we were both playing it cool. I was worried about Andrea, too. Down the track, she would always deny being interested in him, but I think she was rewriting history. I was so convinced that she liked him I was scared to tell her I liked him too, so I kept it to myself. And besides, Bon barely said hello to me over the steaming iron. I didn't think he wanted to know about me either.

Barry McKenzie is what finally brought us together. McKenzie was this comic-book character created by the comedian Barry Humphries - the same guy who does Dame Edna Everage - and he was huge in the Seventies. He was the British stereotype of an ugly Australian, this typical Aussie bogan character who was rough and rude, and spoke in the silliest kind of ocker jargon. I thought he was hilarious (I still do), and for some reason I thought Bon would agree. I bought a copy of 'Bazza Pulls It Off!', the latest Barry McKenzie comic, and dropped into the house in North Adelaide to see who was around.

Julie and Vince might have been there, but it was Bon and I that ended up side by side on the couch, flipping through the book together and laughing our arses off. We were in hysterics reading the 'Glossary of McKenzieisms' at the back of the book. 'Nut-chokers' were underpants; 'snot rag' was a handkerchief; 'up the freckle' meant up the backside. 'Crack a fat' was in there (which means 'get an erection') and so was 'brewer's droop' (which means you're too drunk to get it up). I'll never forget the explanation of 'to slip someone a length', which was 'to fall in love nicely'.

Bon loved 'Bazza Pulls It Off!'. There was something about the Australian-ness of it that really appealed to him; the language was really off but it was also really familiar. Later, when Bon started sending me letters, I could see the same sense of humour in his writing. He had a knack for the vernacular, but it was all tongue in cheek. He didn't write things to be deep and meaningful, he wrote to make you smile. Bon called it his 'toilet poetry'.

Bazza was a real ice-breaker for us. That day in North Adelaide was the first time Bon and I really talked. It was the first time we really laughed together (and he had such a lovely, husky laugh). I felt that nervous spark, that thing you feel when you meet someone and you think it could take off but you're really not sure. I didn't want him to know how much I liked him, but the truth is I liked him a lot. I don't know what Bon thought of me. I wasn't very sure of myself. I was timid, in a lot of ways. I knew I wasn't ugly, but I hardly thought I was beautiful; I just knew that I was a bit different. More than anything, I loved to laugh, and I liked people that made me laugh. Bon made me laugh more than anyone.

31

Back in those days, you didn't meet someone then start emailing them or text-messaging them, you had to wait for fate to throw you together again. Julie and Vince had a bit of scheme, however. They decided we'd all go to the drive-in together.

'Bon wants to know if you'll go out with him,' Julie told me.

I almost jumped out of my seat to say yes.

The next Friday night, the three of them came to pick me up in Vince's car, Julie and Vince in the front and Bon and I sitting next to each other in the back. I opened the door and there he was, with a nervous sort of half smile on his face. He'd obviously made a bit of an effort for our date (or tried to, at least). He was in a khaki-coloured long-sleeve grandpa T-shirt and a tight pair of bell-bottomed jeans. The woven leather headband he was wearing was a bit funny-looking, but it went well with the patchouli oil he'd used for aftershave. (It's not his fault, patchouli oil was big in the Seventies.) I thought his shoes were a bit odd. Bon was wearing these very girly boots, which had a bit of a heel. I found out later they were actually women's boots and that he'd borrowed them from Julie. It was the first of many outfits that I saw him in that made me giggle.

Our date went downhill pretty fast. It was horrible, really, I was that nervous. I had a bad habit with blokes; it was always the ones I didn't like that chased me. If I didn't care what they thought I would be easy-going and quick with a joke, but the minute I actually fancied someone I just froze up. He might as well have been sitting next to a blow-up doll. (He might have seen more action.) Not that Bon was doing any better than me.

The drive-in didn't do us any favours. We should have gone to a bar and had a couple of drinks to grease the wheels, but instead we sat there stiff as boards, staring straight ahead without saying a word to each other. It was painful. I was starting to think I should have brought the old Barry McKenzie out with me, when all of a sudden he lay down across the back seat and put his head in my lap. *What the hell is this?* I thought.

'Scratch my head,' Bon said.

'Scratch your own head!' I told him.

'Nah go on, give it a scratch.'

I scratched his head and it was probably the most awkward five minutes of my life. I had no idea what he was doing. I suppose he was just looking for a window of opportunity, but instead of pulling me over for a kiss, he fell over in my lap. It was pretty weird. I'm sure Bon regretted it the minute he got down there - *What did I do that for?!* – but I was more embarrassed about my reaction than anything else. Anyway, it didn't last long and it didn't go anywhere, if that's what he intended. He sat bolt upright a few minutes later and we watched the rest of the film in virtual silence.

I felt like a terrible idiot, and it only got worse on the way home. Bon complained that he had to go interstate the next day with the band and I turned my nose up at him.

'That's the price of fame,' I said, voice dripping with sarcasm.

I can still hear myself. I was trying to hang shit on him, as they say. I think I meant to be funny or cool, but I just sounded like a dope. I really, really, *really* liked him, but I wasn't doing a very good job of showing it. The whole date was a disaster.

Bon walked me to the front door and very politely said, 'Thank you for coming out with me, Irene.'

Then he turned around and left. My heart sank. *Oh god*, I thought, *I blew it.*

The next day Bon sent me flowers at work, dark red roses. I'd never been given flowers in my life. *Why would he send me flowers?* I thought. *He must be having a laugh.* I was trying to figure out what it meant. I know that sounds ridiculous, but I really didn't want to look stupid. I'd had enough of that the last time around.

I'm not sure how Bon managed to convince me that he was into me, but he convinced me. Don't ask me *why* he was into me. Must have been the Barry McKenzie afterglow. Anyway, I don't think it was that hard. I wanted to be won over.

He started calling me at work and we went out on a few dates, and soon enough we were hanging out regularly. I was back in the public service by then, working for the Civil Aviation Authority in the Da Costa Building on Grenfell Street. The best part of my day was at 5pm when Bon roared up on his little yellow trail bike to pick me up. I'd hike up my little skirt, swing a leg over and we'd be off.

Sometimes we'd ride up to Hemming's Farm and hang out with the guys from Fraternity. I met Sam See, the drummer, and the harmonica player, John Eyers (who everybody called Uncle). Mick Jurd was the guitarist and he was a bit older than the other guys; he lived at the back of the farm in a cottage, along with his wife Carol. They all seemed nice enough. They were a little more intellectual than Bon, but he obviously respected them a lot.

Sometimes we wouldn't go anywhere in particular; we'd just cruise around those winding roads around the Adelaide Hills. Bon loved his bike. He loved to ride fast and he loved to muck around. My brother had motorcycles so I was pretty fearless on the back, not that I really had much to worry about. Bon was more silly than macho. We'd drive through a hot gust of wind and he'd yell out 'Hot tap!', then through a cool patch of air and he'd yell 'Cold tap! Cold tap! Hot tap! Cold tap! Cold tap!' - just to make me laugh.

In the beginning, we were both real smart-arses. We teased and mocked each other all the time. I gave him a hard time about being a musician, and he called me 'The World Traveller' (he was taking the piss). We were both naturally quite defensive and didn't like to let on when we liked someone, so we pretended we didn't like each other *that much* at first. But it didn't last long. Once the two of us relaxed and started being nice to each other, it was really easy-going. Not that we softened completely. One sunny day up at the farm, we were crashed on the grass with a couple of beers, and I was grinning from ear to ear.

'You look really happy,' Bon said to me. 'You've got more wrinkles 'round your eyes than I do.'

One of the biggest things we had in common was music - we talked about it constantly. He loved Free; he was really into Paul Rodgers' voice. Bob Dylan and The Band were always on the stereo up at the farm. I think Fraternity really worshipped them. There was a lot of country and rock 'n' roll floating around, but Bon loved the classics too, rock 'n' roll and swing, even a bit of blues. It wasn't all about the bloke's music either; he dug my Carole King album and we listened to Joni Mitchell together. He even liked jazz. Bon was really curious about the records I had brought back from London, so I took them around to Norwood and we listened to them together. He went crazy for The Sensational Alex Harvey Band. Alex Harvey was a Scot, like Bon, and a real rock 'n' roller. He became one of Bon's idols.

We hung out with Vince and Julie quite a bit, although Andrea made herself scarce when Bon and I started dating. I introduced him to my other friends instead. I knew a group of Chinese students studying at Adelaide Uni, which impressed Bon no end. I think he was impressed by the fact that there were Chinese people in Adelaide, let alone that they were friends of mine - Asian people stood out like sore thumbs back then. But there was nothing awkward about it for Bon. He liked meeting new people, wherever they came from. My friend Soochew (he called himself 'A Boy Named Sue') took us out for a Chinese meal. There were about four Chinese restaurants in town and they were all on the same block, little cafes with Laminex tables and the best home-made food south of Shanghai. It must have been a first for Bon - he went nuts for the crispy fried pork and abalone. He couldn't stop raving about it. He liked Soochew's friends, too. They had a very particular and very quirky sense of humour and Bon dug it almost as much as the food. Soochew used to throw his arms around me and yell 'Chinese bear hug!', then squeeze me until my ribs cracked. He was a great laugh.

Every time we went out for a Chinese meal after that, Bon ordered in a broken Chinese accent.

'I have fry rice, yeah? An, ah, spling roll, yeah?'

I would roll my eyes and laugh at him. He wasn't being racist, he was just trying to fit in, but he went about it in a pretty ridiculous way.

Slowly but surely, we got to know each other. It was easy enough. Bon was so warm and relaxed, and we really loved being in each other's company. The conversation never dried up. I don't know if we talked about anything too serious, but we certainly talked a lot.

There wasn't a trace of a Scottish accent on Bon, although he did a great impression of his Mum. He was true-blue Aussie, but he wasn't rough. And he often played dumb, but he was sharp as a tack. He liked people a lot. He wanted people to like him, too. Bon drank a lot and he liked to have a good time, but could also be really gentle. There was something a little bit hippy about him, but I think it was more a sign of the times than anything else. Bon had been to see a white witch when he lived in Melbourne, a fortune-teller. He didn't say much about it, but he believed in supernatural stuff, which was a surprise given the type of guy he was. He told me he'd once woken up and seen a ghost at the end of his bed, somebody he knew that had died. He said it in a very matter-of-fact way. I didn't know what to think. The fortune-teller told him he'd be close to a blonde woman and a red-headed woman, which sounded quite promising to me.

Bon's fashion sense was all over the place. He got around in band T-shirts and tight jeans but he carried this long, fringed bag over his shoulder, which is where he kept his recorders (Bon played the recorder on a Fraternity tune called 'Seasons of Change'). He always had that hippy bag flopping around on the back of his motorbike. He burned incense, too, and he had candles everywhere. He had a collection of beautiful ornate tiles that he found up at Hemming's Farm that he used as candle-holders. He found a beautiful old clock in the shed at Aldgate, too, a lovely miniature grandfather thing that sits on a mantel-piece. He restored it and gave it to me as a present.

He was talented, but he had a rough edge to him that I really liked - not that he was macho. Bon was a peacemaker; that was his nature. He wouldn't back away from a fight but he didn't go looking for them, although his sense of justice often got him into trouble. There was a night down at the Largs Pier when he went toe-to-toe with the security guards, just because he thought it was the right thing to do. The bouncers were massive, speed-fuelled blokes who delighted in throwing drunken punters out the door, and on this particular night, there were three of them laying into a mouthy drunk. Bon appeared in the doorway and asked them to stop.

'Come on guys, that's enough,' he told them.

These huge guys turned away from the drunk and squared up to Bon, but Bon wasn't scared and he wouldn't walk away. I was sitting in the car with Julie when someone came over and told us that Bon was hurt. There were other girls hanging around outside and the rumour had obviously spread.

'Oh no, not Bon!' they were muttering.

I think women felt protective of him because he was so little. I knew Bon could take care of himself. When he eventually climbed into the car, he had blood all over his T-shirt.

'Honestly,' he grinned at me, 'It wasn't my fault.'

I'd never dated a guy with tattoos before and Bon had a few. Tattoos were unusual back then, not like now. Who doesn't have a tattoo these days? Wharfies and ex-cons had them in the Seventies and they were real back-yard jobs; Bon got most of his in Western Australia when he was working on the docks. He'd had to cover them with make-up when he was singing in The Valentines. He had pictures of daggers and the Scottish coat of arms, but his favourite was the birds he had inked across his pelvis. Bon loved to unzip his jeans and show them to me.

'Do you want to see the branch they're on?' he'd grin.

We'd been dating for ages before we finally did the deed. It felt like ages, anyway. There was a lot of kissing in dark corners at the Largs Pier Hotel, and lots of dates that ended with me getting walked to the front door and deposited there like a box of fragile goods. I was starting to think I smelled funny or something. Then one day, things just went off on a different course.

The Fraternity place in Norwood had two bedrooms at the front of the house: one off to the left, which was Bon's, and one off to the right for Bruce Howe. We were hanging out in Bruce's room one night, talking music and other bullshit, when I got up to go to the toilet. On my way back, just before I made it to Bruce's door, a pair of arms shot out from Bon's doorway and pulled me in the opposite direction. The door slammed shut behind us and away we went.

It was pretty funny, I'll say that much. I don't think I've been flipped around quite so enthusiastically, before or since. It was like the Olympics. *Right, there you go, over you go, I can do that, I can do this.* He was like a little hurricane, swinging from the chandeliers - I actually had no idea what the fuck was going on. Anyway, I'm glad it wasn't like that every night. I think Bon proved whatever he needed to prove that first time and then settled down into slightly more manageable behaviour. The most ridiculous thing I had to put up with after that was when he came out of the shower with a towel hanging over his business parts. That was just Bon though. He'd do anything to make you laugh.

CHAPTER 2

Bon talked about his family quite a lot. He really adored his Mum Isa, and he had been away from home for a long time. He missed her. Isa sent Bon a hamper once, and he sat on the bed with tears in his eyes while he opened it. She sent him biscuits and socks and other Mum-type things (nothing he would have actually wanted) and he was incredibly sentimental about it. The rest of the world knew him as Bon, he said, but he was always Ron to his Mum.

He wasn't soft, he was just decent. When he talked about growing up in Perth, I got a pretty good picture of how much trouble he could be. All of his stories were about drunken escapades and near misses, and Bon being a right little larrikin. He was charged with some bizarre carnal knowledge offence when he was a teenager, and then he got into more trouble later on when he hit a policeman at a local dance. He spent a few months in a juvenile detention centre when he was sixteen, 'at Her Majesty's pleasure', as he liked to say. I think it must have scared him straight - or less crooked, anyway. The Valentines must have been the only teenybopper band in Australia to be charged with marijuana possession.

Bon spoke very highly of his brothers, Derek and Graeme. Graeme was seven years younger than Bon, but he was in the merchant marines so he was quite the world traveller. He found his way to Adelaide often enough to keep Bon happy. Graeme was about eighteen when I met him; very sweet, very gentle and very fond of his older brother. We'd all go out together when Graeme was in town and he would sit quietly in a corner with his beer, looking round at everyone with these big almond eyes and letting out a little giggle every now and then. He was quite shy. Bon was always the life of the party, so it was a wonder the two of them came from the same family, but Graeme was just coming into his own. He was much more confident when he got older.

Bon met my Mum very early on; she lured him in with food. We always had our Sunday roast on a Saturday for some reason, but in every other way it was the Australian classic - big leg of lamb, lovely crispy potatoes and plenty of gravy. I don't know what Mum made of Bon when he first appeared, in skin-tight jeans with tattoos all over the shop, but he had certainly won her over by the time we'd finished eating.

'This is lovely Mrs Thornton!' he kept saying. 'Delicious! I haven't had a decent feed since I left my Mum's place.' The minute he was done licking the plate he leapt to his feet and grabbed a tea towel. 'I'll help with the dishes!'

I was gagging. My mother thought he was an angel.

Bon came round another night for cold meats and beetroot, and something my mother called 'Aussie salad'. He hardly had a forkful into his mouth before he was singing its praises.

'Mrs Thornton, I love beetroot,' he said. 'I could beat it all around the plate.'

I almost laughed out loud. He saved his most corny material for the oldies and they loved it. I met a woman in Perth later on who spoke very fondly of the night when a teenage Bon, a friend of her son, had turned up on her doorstep blind drunk and covered in vomit.

'His pants were so tight we had to cut them off him!' she laughed.

She had a soft spot for Bon, vomit and all.

It made me really nervous that Mum had warmed to Bon so quickly. In the back of my head, I still thought it could all come undone.

'He's just lovely,' my Mum beamed at me one night.

'He's been to jail, you know,' I said. *That'll put a pin in it.*

'Oh has he?' Mum said absent-mindedly. 'He's lovely, though, isn't he?'

Bon had that effect on women. He loved them and they loved him.

He was sitting on the porch in a tight yellow T-shirt the day he met my little sister Fay. Fay came bounding up in her school uniform and Bon broke out in a grin from ear to ear.

'G'day,' he said, 'Who are you?'

Bon always claimed he took the long way home when school got out so he could enjoy the view. It became a bit of a standing joke around our place.

'Can you please change out of your uniform? Bon's coming over.'

God help him if Fay and her friends came home from sports practice in those little pleated skirts. Fay thought he was hilarious; cheeky and warm, but also very kind. He had an artist friend that made T-shirts and he gave her one with a bulldog screen-printed across the front.

'Whaddya think of this?' he said.

Fay screwed up her nose in true teenage girl fashion.

It was embarrassing having to manoeuvre Bon around my family, but they had their uses. If he didn't pick me up from work, I relied on Mum to be the message bearer. She didn't get a phone until the mid-Eighties, so Bon couldn't call me at home. He'd often just turn up at Mum's place, but sometimes I didn't know if he was coming over or not and I didn't like to sit around on a Saturday night hoping I might see him. Better to let him think I was off having a great time.

'I'll be at the British Hotel in North Adelaide, Mum. The British. Have you got that? The BRITISH.'

Mum did her duty and Bon usually found me. I was sitting at the pub by myself one weekend, watching the Moonshine Jug and String Band (who later became The Angels), when two girls came in looking for me.

'Bon asked us to come and get you,' they said.

The girls were sisters, Vicki and Anita. I barely knew them, I just knew that they knew the guys in Fraternity. They bundled me into the back seat of their Volkswagen and drove me out to the Largs Pier, and lovely Bon was waiting for me when we arrived.

There was a pub in North Adelaide called the Hotel Australia, a great glass building with a pool table downstairs and a dance floor upstairs. They had bands on every now and then. Bon picked me up after work one day and we headed over there to meet the rest of the gang - Vince and Julie, and the guys from Fraternity. Bon must have had a meal or two during the day, but I certainly hadn't. There was no stopping for food though, it was straight into the beer. The guys played pool. Drink after drink appeared on the table in front of me and sure enough, the room soon started to swim. Everyone else was in great form, belting out Rod Stewart's 'Maggie May' at the top of their lungs.

'You right, 'Rene?' Bon asked, and I nodded weakly.

I must have slid out of my seat at some point and made my way to the toilet because I found myself slumped against the cubicle wall with my eyes closed. *I'm pissed*, I thought, *I'm horribly pissed*. I was going to throw up. I managed to pull myself together long enough to sneak outside and around the corner, where no one could see me, and pour myself into a cab. At home, my poor Mum opened the door to a daughter who could barely stand up. She was meek though, my lovely Mum, and she didn't give me a hard time.

'If Bon comes round,' I told her, 'Don't let him in!'

Mum ran to get me a bucket in case I was sick and I made my way to the bedroom, and sure enough just minutes later I heard Bon's bike pulling up outside. I could hardly keep myself on the bed, I was so drunk. God knows why, but Mum let him into the house. He stuck his head around the bed-room door, and right at that second my stomach heaved and I threw up. Bon, bless him, was very sympathetic. He just sat down beside me and held my hair out of the way.

'You're alright love,' he said. 'Better out than in.'

I was sick as a dog but I had one clear thought in my head. I was going to kill my Mum the minute I could stand upright. I was mortified.

The Hotel Australia was the scene of many crimes. On more than one night, Bon tore up the dance floor while I sat on the sidelines shaking my head. I rarely got up with him because I just couldn't dance. He caught me at it one night at the Largs Pier, where it was so dark I thought I was safe.

'That was really good,' he laughed. 'Fast fast, slow slow slow, fast fast, slow slow slow. I could almost see you counting out loud.'

Cheeky bastard.

Fay came out with us to the Australia one night and she swore she'd never dance with Bon again after that. They went out on to the dance floor together and then suddenly he was off, going solo. He left her stranded. Bon needed some-one to walk out on to the floor with him so he didn't look like a total dickhead (not that he'd really care), then he was off on a one-man show. He could really dance. He liked a bit of a strut, but he could waltz and do that old rock 'n' roll stuff, too. He loved all of it. He just loved to have a good time. He could whip a good time out of thin air.

He could whip up trouble just as easily. Things got a bit out of hand on yet another night at the Australia when Bon got into a fight over money at the pool table. It ramped up very quickly. A big, rough bloke had picked Bon up and was about to throw him across the room when I jumped into the fray and stubbed my cigarette out on the back of the big guy's neck. It was honestly the first thing that came into my head - not the most sophisticated tactic but it did the job. Bon was dropped on his arse and we practically ran out of there.

Bon wasn't very aggressive but he got into trouble when he was drinking. He was reckless with the booze, even back then, although I did my fair share of young, dumb things. We rode back from a party at Aldgate one night and I was dead drunk on the back of the bike, sliding off to one side and then the other. Bon kept reaching back to scoop me up, first the left then the right, then the left then the right, *woops, woops, woops.* Mind you, he was probably drunk too. He was often pissed when he rode. More than once I saw him park his bike right up on the veranda of his house and climb in through the bedroom window with his helmet on.

Bon was a risk-taker, it was just his nature. Whether it was booze or drugs or motorbikes, or anything else that took his fancy, he just waded in with a grin on his face. Most of the time, it worked out just fine, but he gave me a scare every now and then. We were at a Fraternity show in the country one day, out at the Riverland Festival near Berri. Right after the band finished playing (on the back of a flatbed truck), Bon climbed the nearest tree and dove straight into the river. My heart stopped. Anyone with half a brain wouldn't do something like that. Bon couldn't stop himself.

It was strange being with someone in a band. Girls had always fancied Bon, and that didn't stop when he started going out with me. He was muscular and strong, and Fraternity had a big following; he had no shortage of admirers. Even Fay's friends from school went to see them - they'd corner her after the show and giggle about Bon, who looked like a giant up there on stage. (He was actually shorter than me by a couple of inches, but it didn't seem to bother him. I think his confidence made him seem taller than he actually was.)

I would find myself in the toilet at a gig listening to girls talk about how they'd hung out with Bon the night before or they'd seen him around here or there. I didn't know what it meant. If he was sleeping around, I didn't know about it. I sometimes wondered if they knew I was his girlfriend and were trying to wind me up. I wondered if they were jealous. More than anything, I just worried that I was on shaky ground, because Bon was so popular and I felt so ordinary in comparison. But in the end, I chose to ignore it. If I'd been any less naïve, I'm sure it would have been a problem.

There was a girl called Margaret Smith hanging around Adelaide at the time who used to give me the evil eye. She obviously had some sort of issue with me, but I couldn't figure out what it was. Bon and I were at a festival one day when he laid out a blanket for the two of us, but as soon as it hit the ground, Margaret appeared and sat down on it. She stared at me, gave me a dark look, and then just stared at Bon without saying a word. I thought she was mad. Years later, I read that she and Bon had been sleeping together in Adelaide some time in the early Seventies; she was married to another bloke, but she would crawl in through Bon's bedroom window every now and then. I don't know if this was going on when Bon and I were together. It might have been earlier and it might not, I don't know. I was blissfully unaware at the time.

I had my reasons for trusting Bon, even if they were a bit misguided. He never flirted with other women in front of me, not seriously. He was always very affectionate towards me, despite all these other women that were floating around. We were in the middle of a pretty intense romance. He paid me a lot of attention, especially at gigs, where he'd get off the stage and make a beeline for me in the crowd. He made me feel like I was the only person in the room.

Years later, I was painted as this frosty princess who thought I was better than everyone else; this worldly, exotic girl who had flown in from London and caught Bon's eye because I was hard to get. I laughed out loud when I read that about myself, and so would anyone who knew me back then. I was no mystery woman. I was a twenty-year-old with a bit of a hard shell, but I was still very innocent. Bon and I just clicked. I had an odd little brain - it was always ticking over - and I think Bon was similar to me in that way. I don't know. It's hard to explain why we fell for each other. We just did.

Bon was so lovely to me for such a long time that it came as a real shock when he slipped. We were heading to the Pooraka Hotel in the middle of winter one night, four or five months after we'd first met. The Pooraka was like all those suburban beer barns in the Seventies, full of smoke and sweaty, stinky people all having a good time. You were lucky if you could get a table. Most people stood around in clumps or pushed their way down to the front of the stage to watch the band. You were guaranteed a good night out there.

I'd gone to a lot of effort with my black suede boots and black velvet jacket, make-up and hair and all the rest, but Bon didn't notice.

The only thing he said when I arrived at his place was, 'Get around to the other side of the room and help me make the bed.'

Then later at the pub, he just ignored me. For the first time since we'd started dating, it was like I wasn't there. He was drinking and having a laugh, talking to everyone and anyone but me. It wasn't that big of a deal in the scheme of things, but I remember the feeling really well. It was a really lonely feeling. I felt like the third wheel in a relationship between Bon and the rest of the world. He had this big personality, and I could see how much people loved being around him, but it was like he was standing in a spotlight surrounded by his fans and I was watching from the sidelines. It was the first time I had ever felt that way around him, and to this day I don't know why it happened. I don't even think there was a reason, he was just having a brilliant time with his mates. If I was really confident, deep down, I probably wouldn't even have noticed, but at that point in my life

44

I felt like I was invisible if Bon didn't see me.

I celebrated my twenty-first birthday in December 1971. Bon and Bruce Howe picked me up after work to take me to the pub for a birthday pint. Bon was in the back seat with my birthday present in his hands.

'Happy birthday,' he smiled, and leaned over to dump his very heavy parcel in my lap.

I unwrapped it and started to laugh. It was pretty bizarre. He had given me one half of a pair of candles that were cast models of his legs and feet, made by the girlfriend of a friend of his. Bon kept one and gave me the other one for my birthday, starting years of jokes about how I had stolen his foot. He knew it would make me giggle.

I had a couple of drinks at the Hotel Australia before announcing that I had to go. I was having a family do at the Enfield Hotel with my mum and my sisters.

'Why didn't you invite me?' Bon asked.

We had been going out for months and months by then, but it just didn't occur to me. I would never have dreamed of asking The Bastard along to something like that because it would have been horrible. He would have spent the whole night looking down his nose at us.

'I didn't think you'd like that sort of thing,' I told Bon. 'It's going to be terrible. Ernie Sigley is performing.'

Ernie Sigley was a comedian who sang songs, or a singer who told really corny jokes between tunes. He was quite well known, but he was strictly for the oldies. I really couldn't see rock 'n' roll Bon getting into it.

'Nah, I'd love to come,' he grinned.

Kathleen's husband Barry was supposed to be there but he couldn't make it for some reason, and I knew Mum had booked for four people. I told Bon he was welcome. I was sure he'd be bored, but of course Bon Scott was never bored. He made his own fun.

The Ernie Sigley thing was basically just dinner and a show; people eating their meat and three veg while Ernie roamed about with a microphone. He chatted with the audience, told awful, cheesy jokes and led the crowd in big sing-a-long numbers. It was the most uncool thing I'd ever seen and I was cringing the whole time. Not Bon, though. He was right in there, singing and laughing, and clapping along. You've never seen such enthusiasm for dinner theatre. I think he went over and above, just to show my family what a good sport he was (such a terrible, terrible suck-up). And when he decided to enjoy something, he didn't do it by halves.

Kathleen met Bon for the first time that night. She adored him just as much as Mum did, which is funny because she and I didn't always get along that well. She fell under Bon's spell, just like everyone else, and the two of them remained very good friends for years.

On Christmas Eve, Fraternity played at the Pooraka Hotel. It was a good night (we all got a bit drunk), but when Mick and Carol drove me home, it descended into a bit of a row. I was never good at giving directions and I'd taken them down a few dead ends, which was really embarrassing. I apologised to them, but Carol's patience was obviously pretty thin.

She turned around and started yelling at me, 'I got hit in the head with a cymbal tonight and I just want to get home, for god's sake.'

Mick had a few unkind things to say, one of which involved the word 'moll'. I was completely shocked. I didn't know these guys all that well and they were being unnecessarily harsh. Bon was in the back seat beside me and he didn't say a word. Mick was supposed to take him home after he dropped me off, but Bon jumped out of the car at my place and slammed the door behind him. It was his way of saying *fuck you*.

So Bon ended up staying at my place on Christmas Eve of 1971. Mum was away in Port Pirie for the holidays and it was just Fay and I in the house, conveniently enough. Fay had a boy over and they were sleeping in our bedroom, so Bon and I had no choice but to sleep in Mum's room. What a sacrilege that was. My Mum wasn't Catholic, but she had a lot of religious paraphernalia around the room. Little saints and angels watched over us while we did the deed in my mother's bed.

The next morning I snuck outside and cut a rose from the bush in the front yard. I had bought Bon a bottle of brandy for Christmas and I wanted to dress it up a little bit. I didn't want to look like I was making too much of an effort, but I thought the flower was a subtle romantic gesture. I don't think Bon gave me anything that year, other than a cuddle. I told Bon I loved him for the very first time that morning. 'That's just as well,' he laughed.

Later, there was a knock on the front door and I got up to find our neighbour Doris peering in the front window. She had popped over to give Fay and I our Christmas presents, which for some unknown reason were giant white granny pants. It was brilliant. The timing couldn't have been better because it gave Bon something to laugh about for the rest of the day. They were no sooner out of the packet than he had them on and stretched right up to his chin, and he was running around the house like a baby in an over-sized nappy.

He was in a merry mood that Christmas, fuelled by the brandy. It brought out the absolute worst in him. Fay had a couple of friends drop round and Bon was driving them nuts.

'Hey Fay, check it out!' he said. He came bouncing backwards through the lounge room, completely naked with his penis flapping behind him like a tail.

'Skippy the Bush Kangaroo!' he shouted, bouncing out through another door.

Honestly, he was so embarrassing. I couldn't help but giggle.

As Fay and her friends were filing out the front door, Bon called to her from the bedroom.

'Hey Fay!' he yelled, and they all looked over to see Bon, upside down with his legs in the air, flashing them his bum hole. Fay's mates let out a wave of gasps and cleared out as fast as their legs would carry them. Bon laughed so hard he almost cried. I stood in the doorway, laughing at him laughing so hard, and rolling my eyes as far back as they would go.

This is it, I thought to myself. *This is the man for me.*

CHAPTER 3

Bon was happy in Fraternity. The guys in the band were more sophisticated than him, but he really looked up to them. They were all very deep, university educated, and in comparison Bon was really rough and ready, but he was no dummy. What he lacked in sophistication he made up for with pure charisma. He was happy moulding himself into that scene. They were truly excellent musicians, and that was important for Bon. He could escape all that bubblegum crap that had gone on with The Valentines and started playing serious music.

Fraternity played to packed rooms virtually every weekend in Adelaide. They travelled to Sydney and Melbourne regularly for shows, but there were plenty of empty hours in the day. I think the daylight hours were spent smoking dope and talking shit, biding their time until they became rich and famous. They were pretty cocky, although it didn't seem that far-fetched at the time. The band had been doing really well in Sydney and 'Seasons of Change' went to number one on the local chart; Bon's painted face had been on the cover of Sound Blast magazine and Channel 9 had made a TV show about the band.

I went in to the station with them when they filmed a performance of their single, 'If You Got It' (which had a good groove, and sounded a bit like Canned Heat). I was walking down the corridor with Bon when he stopped and opened a random door. There was a bunch of surprised people inside. Bon turned around, stuck his arse through the door and farted unceremoniously, then closed the door behind him.

'What did you do that for?!' I asked.

'They deserved it,' he laughed.

The rest of them may not have expressed it with their arses, but everyone in Fraternity had a massive ego. There was never any doubt that they would make it big one day. In the meantime, Hamish kept everybody fed and watered. As well as paying their rent and board, he gave the guys a small allowance.

'The Golden Eagle is shitting tomorrow,' Bon would crow.

For long stretches between pay days, he was broke. Bon wasn't above asking me to buy a beer or two, or beer for one of the boys, but

I didn't mind. He didn't make much of a living, but his job seemed more normal to me than being a bank clerk or working at the tax office. He made my life more interesting. He didn't do much for my career, mind you. All the partying and late nights didn't help my shorthand; some days I'd be so knackered I'd have to sneak off to the sick bay and have a little lie down.

Bon had had a few jobs here and there before we met. He had been a postie back in Fremantle and once worked at a place called Avery Scales, as an apprentice weighing- machine mechanic. He also worked on the crayfish boats back in Western Australia. (He told a journalist years later that he'd gotten his ear pierced on a crayfishing boat: 'Just put a spike through it!' he growled. God, that made me laugh.) A nine-to-five job just didn't suit him. He was going to be a rock star, and that was that.

Fraternity were actually quite isolated in Adelaide, but they still thought they were the best band in Australia, and they were convinced they'd be massive if they moved overseas. They beat out Sherbet to win the Hoadley's National Battle of the Sounds competition in 1971 and the prize was a free trip to England. After that, it was all they could talk about. The longer Bon and I were together, the more likely it seemed that he was going to leave. There wasn't much I could do about it. He would go and I'd just have to deal with it. I wasn't going to chase another guy halfway round the world.

By January 1972, the move was definite. Fraternity would be gone in a matter of weeks.

'I want you to come,' Bon told me.

'Well I don't want to,' I said.

'But what are we gonna do?'

'That'll be it,' I told him. 'We'll just leave it and see what happens when you come back.'

The truth is I was devastated, but I didn't want him to know. Bon had his own feelings and his own plans. He told me he was going to ask Hamish to pay for my fare to England. Hamish had struck a deal with the band; wives would get a free trip to England, but not girlfriends. Bon asked him to make an exception for me. He picked me up after work and took me home, and the two of us sat on the fence outside of Mum's place, talking it over.

'You have to come now, 'Rene,' he told me. 'I've arranged everything.'

I was nervous, but I knew he loved me. I nodded and he grinned, and gave me a huge smack on the lips.

'I was gonna ask you to marry me, but I thought you'd run a mile,' he said.

I felt a bit light-headed.

'But I wouldn't have.'

Bon smiled.

'Are you serious?' he said, and I nodded. 'Well... will ya?'

I don't remember what I said next, but it had the word 'yes' in it.

'Hold on one second,' Bon told me. 'I've got to ask your Mum.'

We practically bowled Mum over as we ran into the house.

'Mrs Thornton, I want to marry your daughter,' Bon grinned.

My mother looked up at him, and in her sweet little voice said, 'Are you sure?'

'Jesus, Mum!' I laughed. 'What's wrong with me?'

That was one mother out of the way. Bon had to find a phone box next and call Isa in Perth. I could hear her heavy Scottish brogue crackling down the line from Fremantle.

'Mum, 'Rene and me are getting married!' he said, and then he laughed. 'No Mum, she's not pregnant. She's on the little white ones.'

We went to Largs Pier that night and Bon told everyone he talked to that we were getting married, and there were plenty of drinks and slaps on the back to celebrate. I didn't notice anyone else, only him. If there were other girls around, I didn't notice. I was too happy. Bon was happy. We were a proper little pair of romantic idiots that night, with king-sized crushes on each other and a bright future in London to look forward to. I'd never really thought about getting married, but if I was going to do it, there was only one man for the job.

I became Mrs Bon Scott on January 24, 1971, about two weeks after he proposed. The only thing that slowed us down was having to wait for Bon's birth certificate to arrive from Scotland. *The faster the better*, I thought. I didn't want him to change his mind.

It was a bit of a marrying season for Fraternity. John Freeman and his seventeen-year-old girlfriend Anita had a church wedding just a few weeks before Bon and I, but we decided to do it at the registry office. It seemed like the sensible option, quick and easy, without having to book a venue and all the rest of that nonsense. I never wanted a white wedding and Bon didn't care; he was happy if I was happy.

My relatives drove in for the day, Auntie Nell and my gran, and my older brother Peter and his wife Rosie. Peter was a metallurgist who worked at the smelting plant in Port Pirie. He had met Bon briefly before the wedding. (Bon pulled up in a car with a few of the guys from Fraternity when Peter and I were standing out the front of Mum's place.

'Who's JC in the front seat?' Peter asked, because one of the guys had a beard.) Peter was a no bullshit kind of guy with a very dry wit. I loved him a lot. Bon met Peter's wife Rosie on our wedding day, a German woman with brown hair and a lovely big smile.

'Phwoar, she's alright,' Bon winked at me.

It didn't bother him in the least that we were about to get married.

Isa had flown in from Perth. I had met her once, at a Fraternity gig at the Largs Pier. Bon warned me she'd be there and I wanted to make a good impression, so I wore my longest skirt, a nice checked shirt, my best manners and my biggest smile. I shouldn't have worried - Isa was an easy-going woman. She would never size you up. She loved to chat and she had a really infectious laugh; a trim woman with a thick Scottish accent and a lovely, angular face. She was full of life, just like Bon.

Isa and my Mum went to the same hairdresser before the wedding and they both came back with the same hairdos - they looked like a pair of ice-cream cones. They must have asked for the Queen Elizabeth.

The whole wedding party was being driven around in Fraternity's tour bus, an old Fifties-style Greyhound with silver panelling and blue vinyl seats. Bob Noble, the Fraternity roadie, was our chauffeur. He pulled up front of Mum's place that morning with a symphony of air brakes and a tour bus full of old ladies. Isa and Bon were on board, plus a few of my extended family members; Mum and I were the last to be collected.

Bon jumped out of the bus to say good morning, wearing the only suit he owned, which he'd nicked from a shop in town (or so he said). It was a shit brown colour with wide lapels - you couldn't get more Seventies if you tried. It didn't matter to me if he was wrapped in tin foil.

'You look like a spunk,' he said, kissing me on the cheek.

I was wearing a Forties-style cream dress. It was made from this beautiful crepe material, with a long skirt and a split right up the front, little covered buttons and a matching jacket. I found it in Julie's dress shop, but it looked like a proper wedding outfit, more or less. I had nicked down to the florist and bought a little rose garland to pin to the front, but I skipped the bouquet. My hair must have been gleaming; I rinsed it in rainwater about four-thousand times that morning.

Isa had given me a gold chain with a little pearl on it to wear at the wedding. Bon knew it wasn't my kind of thing but I was wearing it to please his Mum.

'Thanks 'Rene,' he whispered in my ear.

I jumped on to the bus with Bon and eased myself on to a vinyl seat, saying g'day to the family. My Auntie Beth was on board, along with my cousin. She'd met Bon for the first time that morning.

'I like him a lot better than the last one,' she told me.

My tiny grandmother was on the Greyhound as well, completely unfazed by the state of it. We hadn't done anything to the bus; the band's gear was still in the racks overhead, along with Bon's worn, old denim jacket. It was all very relaxed. Well, everyone else was relaxed. I was a great big pile of nerves. Someone took a picture of me, surrounded by the oldies, looking lovely and serene in my wedding clothes, and the next second I was screaming out the bus window.

'Hurry up Mum, for fuck's sake!'

She was still fiddling around in the house, looking for her gloves. I didn't want to be late for my own wedding.

January can be stinking hot in Adelaide but we got lucky; it was bright and mild. We pulled up out front of the Adelaide Town Hall and piled off of the bus, stopping for a photo at the entrance to civic hall. There was a plaque to the left of the door that said

'Births, Deaths and Marriages', and one to the right that said 'Poultry and Apiary'.

'I'm here to marry my chick,' Bon announced.

There was a plain room to one side of the registry desk lined with chairs and it was chock-a-block. All the guys from Fraternity were there with their girlfriends, plus everyone I knew. Fay and her boyfriend were down the front with Kathleen and her husband, my aunts and cousins. Aside from the oldies in the front row, it wasn't too formal - plenty of the younger crowd were in jeans. It was more of a party atmosphere than anything else, with jokes and banter bouncing around the room.

John Bisset and Bruce Howe were there as our witnesses, sharing the best man duties. There was no maid of honour or bridesmaids, just a couple of plain, white gold rings that we'd picked up in the city the week before. There was no grand entrance. Bon and I walked in, said hello to a few people and sat down in the front row while we waited for the justice of the peace to arrive. I was a wreck. Bon seemed pretty relaxed. We stood up again as the celebrant entered the room.

'I see Irene's managed to make herself look taller than Bon again,' someone muttered, and the room erupted in laughter.

I didn't think of Bon as short, but I had heels on under my long dress and I had a few inches on him that day.

The ceremony was very formal but it didn't last long. There were more sniggers when the celebrant read out my middle name, which was the standard reaction. Bon looked very serious while he said his vows, but broke into a huge grin when the JP declared us man and wife.

'Come down here and give me a kiss,' he laughed.

There was clapping and cheering, and a rain of confetti when we walked outside that stuck to my hair and make-up. An older man from the local church came to pay his respects. I thought he was a nice guy and he'd been a great support to my Mum when my father died. He used to call me his favourite blonde, and I called him my favourite pom. Just as we made it out the door of the registry office, he had a quiet word in my ear.

'You know you're not really married in the eyes of the Lord,' he said.

Ey?! I thought, *Who asked you?* I felt pretty bloody married at the time.

We took a few photos on the steps of the town hall, then the whole wedding party clambered back on to the bus and headed over to the house in Norwood. Mick Jurd lined family and friends up against the fence in the back yard for a few more snaps, we had a few drinks, then it was back on to the bus and off to Hemming's Farm for a proper party.

The farm didn't usually host so many oldies, but there were quite a few of them so they kept themselves entertained. The rest of us went about our usual business; music, dancing, dope and laughter. The boys had organised a massive jukebox and rock 'n' roll was roaring out of the windows when we arrived. My Mum, who would revert back to being thirteen years old at the drop of a hat, broke out in mindless dancing the minute we got off the bus. I gripped her shoulders and steered her towards a chair.

'Sit down, Mum,' I told her. 'For god's sake.'

Hamish paid for the catering and my dear Mum supplied the booze, and there seemed to be plenty of both. We had a couple of kegs of beer and a bucket load of spirits, and caterers weaving with platters around the increasingly drunk guests. There was a wedding cake sitting on the table with candles either side, and one of the catering girls managed to set her pigtail on fire as she tried to light them. Just as we were tucking into the food, a yell erupted from the crowd.

'The keg's gone in the dam!'

Half a dozen blokes jumped into the water to rescue the booze. The rest of us were in stitches. Late in the afternoon, while the old ladies sat nattering on the porch, some of our friends had climbed up on to the roof to smoke joints and talk shit. They had a clear view down the hill to water, where some other wedding guests had stripped completely naked and jumped in for a swim.

The whole Fraternity crew was there, including Pat Pickett and a bloke called Tinsley. The two of them didn't seem to have official jobs but they were always hanging around. They helped Fraternity with the gear, I think. Pat later became a roadie for AC/DC. They were a bit like the court jesters those two, always talking in rhyming slang.

'Is this your one another?' Pat said, when he met my brother Peter.

Bon wandered around, checking on his guests. He raised his glass for every toast and snuck the odd drag of a spliff from one of the boys, and made sure Mum and Isa were happy and their drinks were always full. If the ladies noticed the party getting rowdier around them, they didn't say a thing about it. They were happy to sit and let the entertainment come to them. It was balmy and bright and lovely, and most of the crowd stayed on the happy side of their booze. My brother got really smashed and wanted to drive home, but Bon stepped in to talk him out of it. Peter was taking one step towards the car and two steps back, getting closer and closer to the dam as he went. Bon was in stitches, but he still managed the responsible thing. He told Peter there was plenty of room in the house, took his keys and told him to sleep it off.

I barely spoke to Bon at the party, with the endless line of people waiting to give me a hug or share a drink. I got a little pat or a little peck as we passed each other, but we didn't sit down together until Vytas took our picture. Our friend Vytas Serelis was an artist and professional photographer. He took some beautiful shots of Bon and I as the sun went down, sitting side by side on a tree stump towards the back of the farm. We both looked so young and calm. Bon was clean-shaven and his hair was almost as long as mine, but it suited him. He scrubbed up well in his shirt and vest, and he had the loveliest expression on his face. *What a handsome husband*, I thought to myself. Later, when Andrea and I crashed out on a bed surrounded by coats and handbags, she asked me if I was happy. I just smiled.

At the end of the night, or the beginning of the next day, we piled back on to the bus and Bob took us down through the winding hills, back towards the city. The air brakes screamed outside of Bon's place in Norwood and the two of us made to exit, saying our goodbyes. Mum decided it was time for a sex-education talk, but she couldn't work up the nerve.

'Look after your husband,' she said in a very small voice.

I blushed about forty shades of purple. *Bit late for that, Mum.*

We were still on a high when we tumbled into the house. Bon dug through the wedding presents, looking for the gift from our friend Ron Alphabet (so called because we couldn't pronounce his Polish surname). Ron had given us a bottle of Dimple Scotch and my husband wanted a nightcap. He poured half the bottle into my glass. We pushed the presents off the bed, curled up beside each other and talked about everything that had happened that day. At some point, loaded with scotch and completely knackered, the bride and groom passed out.

The wedding day was one of the best days of my life. I know that sounds corny, but it was just perfect. There's nothing better than being in love and having a great big party to celebrate, and I thought Bon was a pretty excellent choice of husband. When we were together, we were in our own little world. Conversation was easy and we had a lot of fun. There just wasn't much depth to it. I was twenty-one and he was twenty-five, and I don't think we ever thought hard about the future. We certainly didn't talk about it. We were too young for mortgages and picket fences - and even if we weren't, we weren't picket-fence sort of people.

Bon was convinced he was going to be famous. I wasn't convinced he was going to be much of anything, I was just happy to be with him. I was happy with the banter and the good times and the lovely little twinkle in his eye when he came to bed. And I think I thought it would last forever, and things would never change.

I woke up the day after the wedding with a cracking hangover. Bon and I went over to Mum's to collect my things and move them over to the Norwood place, although we wouldn't be there long. We were due to leave for England in May. The band was champing at the bit to get away, but they had a few things to get through beforehand, including a regional tour of South Australia. They had a grant from the Arts Council for the tour, which was meant to bring some rock 'n' roll to the bush.

That tour was the closest we got to a honeymoon, piling
on to the bus with the guys from Fraternity, their roadies,
wives and girlfriends to drive to a shitty motel room in a
shitty outback town. We had just landed in Whyalla, a
dustbowl about four hours north-east of Adelaide, when I
realised that we were all expected to share a room. I wanted
a room alone with Bon but there was no chance; I was told
off for making unreasonable demands and all sorts of
bickering followed. Bruce Howe pulled me aside and gave
me a lecture about how tough things would be when we got
to England. There was no room for princesses. I had to pull
my head in, for the good of the band.

Bon was apologetic; he liked playing the good husband. A
guy came to the door at the Norwood place one day looking
for his wayward daughter.

'Sorry mate,' Bon told him. 'Just me and the missus
inside.'

I overheard him from the bedroom and snorted. *The
missus.* We were living in a shared house and having a good
time, and I couldn't quite wrap my head around the Ma and
Pa Kettle thing. The idea of being someone's *missus* seemed
ridiculous. Bon liked the sound of it though; it made him
smile. He just really liked being married. When we pulled up
beside a car on the bike and caught both of our rings
shining in the reflection, we'd hold up our hands at the same
time and say 'Gleam!!', as though we were describing
something in a comic strip.

'I s'pose you'll be six months pregnant and we'll still be
riding around on a motorbike,' Bon laughed.

He took me for a ride up to Margaret Smith's house after
the wedding, at the place she shared with her husband
somewhere up in the hills. Looking back, it must have been a
kind of victory lap for him. At the time, I was just confused.
I really had no idea why we were there. I didn't know her
and I didn't think Bon knew her that well. The conversation
was polite but awkward, and the visit was short. Margaret
walked us to the gate and waved us goodbye, and Bon
didn't mention her again.

Being married didn't stop Bon from partying. He was curled up in the back yard in Norwood one evening after a particularly hard day of drinking and I had to ask Pat Pickett to help me drag him inside.

'Bed time, mate,' I told him, and Pat and I grabbed an arm each, hoisted Bon to his feet and started walking him towards the house.

'Just a minute, just a minute, just a minute,' he slurred. 'What is it?'

'Hold on one sec,' he said, and staggered back towards the lawn. We thought he had left something behind, but he plonked himself back down on the ground, curled up into a ball and immediately started snoring. Even when he was rat shit, he could still make you laugh. We left him out there. He came creeping into bed when he got cold enough.

I had a bit of a job learning how to be a good housewife. I managed to make the washing machine overflow, and Bon had to teach me how to iron his shirts. I don't think I'd touched an iron in my life. I tried to iron the sheets we had gotten as wedding gifts but John's wife Cheryl (who wasn't the nicest woman I'd ever met) turned her nose up at me.

'Mrs Scott irons her sheets,' she sneered.

Are you not supposed to iron sheets? I wondered. Apparently *jeans* needed to be ironed but not bed sheets.

I did my best, but Bon didn't expect much. He had always been pretty independent and he could manage most things better than me. I couldn't cook to save myself. Bon had to show me how to make coleslaw one night (for some reason his version included grated cheese). But I pulled my weight. I went to work every day for one thing, which is more than I could say for my husband.

Bon always seemed to have something to do - it's not like I'd go to work and leave him lying in bed - I'm just not sure what it was. *Band stuff.* The band was rehearsing a lot ahead of the move to England. They spent a few days in the studio in January and recorded a new album, Flaming Galah, which included a song about Hemming's Farm. Bon wrote another tune for the album called 'Welfare Boogie', which was a joke about how he couldn't get a job if he wanted one *(har har)*.

'If You Got It' had done well in South Australia - I heard it on the radio a lot - but the rest of the country hadn't paid much attention. The feeling in Sydney and Melbourne, where it mattered, was that Fraternity had started to go off the boil. The band wasn't at the Sunbury Music Festival in January, where all the other big acts had played, and the album they put out in 1971 (Livestock) hadn't set the world on fire. The guys were oblivious. From where we were standing, their careers were still rolling along pretty nicely. They still had a huge following in Adelaide.

I took Mum down to the Largs Pier one night to hear Bon play and it was as crowded as ever. She twirled around in her odd fashion and I did my best to ignore her. She managed to get my attention anyway. I found her in the bathroom trying to convince two young girls she was in with the band.

'I'm Bon's mother-in-law!' Mum told them.

I dragged her out of there, choking on my embarrassment.

After the regional tour, the band played a couple of big shows with a singer called Jeannie Lewis and the Melbourne Symphony Orchestra for the Adelaide Festival of Arts. Bon was really over the moon about it when he got home. He described the symphony musicians in their black tails, standing and bowing to him in his denim jeans and boots. He thought it was hilarious. I didn't go. I'm sure they were great, but I wasn't interested in being the rock star's wife, I hated that sort of thing. I would never have survived it later on, when Bon got really big. The band did a mini tour of the East Coast in March and I stayed home for that one too.

March 5, 1971

Dear Irene,

Bon's got a sore arm. He had his second shot this afternoon, now he's very sick. He's also very lonely and he misses his beautiful young spouse with all his heart. He's really looking forward to coming home to her 'cause he loves her very much. In fact he told me this morning that there's no one in the whole wide world he loves more and you can bet he's telling the truth 'cause he would never tell a lie (honest) to me 'cause next to you I'm his best friend. He also asked me to say g'day to his favourite mother and sister-in-law. He says that they're the best ones he's ever had. Anyhow, I'd better go now before he finds me writing to you and gets insane by jealousy.

A secret admirer XXXXXXXXXXXXX

When he got back from the tour Bon said, 'I've brought my balls home in a wheelbarrow!', which was his charming way of telling me he'd been faithful.

'Welfare Boogie' came out as a single in late March and Flaming Galah was released in April. It didn't chart or get much radio play because nothing Fraternity recorded really lived up to their live show, but the band ignored it as much as anyone else. By the time it was released, it was all eyes on England. It didn't matter what happened in Australia because Fraternity were going to take over the world.

Uncle's girlfriend Vicki was the only girl who came to London who had to pay her own fare.

'Even the bloody dog got a free fare,' she complained.

Along with his wife Cheryl and their son Brent, John

Bisset brought the family dog, Clutch. Hamish organised big metal trunks for all the couples to pack up their stuff and ship it across - bedding and clothes, kettles and toasters. It was cheaper to take our wedding gifts with us than replace that stuff overseas.

Bon and I moved back in with Mum before we left, when the lease was up on the Norwood place. We slept on two little divans that had been pushed together, in the bedroom that Fay and I used to share. Fay moved into Mum's room and Mum slept on a small bed right at the back of the house.

'I don't think she wants to hear you two having sex,' Fay giggled.

Mum thought she heard a prowler one night and knocked on our door to ask Bon if he would investigate.

'I'm so sorry to bother you,' she told him.

'That's alright,' Bon said, putting on his shorts and emerging from the bedroom. 'Nothing much happening in there anyway.'

He never complained about living with my Mum, though he'd been out of home for a long while. He and Mrs Thornton got on very well. We weren't there long, anyway. The Fraternity couples started taking off, with Hamish, Bon and I bringing up the rear. When everyone else had left, Hamish took us out for a farewell dinner (and we made the most of the free grog and food). It was a Greek restaurant where they danced and smashed plates, and of course Bon got right into it. He was happily pissed and smashing away. *Crash, crash, crash.*

The next morning, he asked me how we'd gotten home.

'You drove!' I told him.

Bon peeked out the window and saw the ute Hamish had loaned us parked at a right angle to the footpath. He looked very sheepish but shrugged his shoulders.

'Must have been a great night,' he laughed.

CHAPTER 4

We left Adelaide in early June 1972. I was even more confident than the last time I'd left town because I was with Bon. I also knew what to expect. I wasn't overly enthusiastic about going back to London but I wasn't upset about it. It was out of my control. I just felt like I was on safe ground in Adelaide, and meeting Bon had made the whole place bearable again. I didn't know what was waiting for me overseas - if I'd known, I would never have gotten on the plane.

Bon was excited. I told him how easy it was to get around London and we laughed about all the English quirks, like drinking warm beer and being too polite. I told him that Brits loved queues.

'If you stop to tie your shoes, people will start lining up behind you.'

I told him what he'd get for his money; that twenty cents was worth about two bob and two bob would buy you a beer in one of the lovely old English pubs. Like everything else in his life, Bon was ready to jump in headfirst. But the adventure for him wasn't really about seeing another country. He was convinced that Fraternity was going to knock them dead in England. The British music we knew was The Rolling Stones, Rod Stewart and Alex Harvey, The Beatles and Led Zeppelin and Free. There was no reason why Fraternity wouldn't fit right in.

We flew three hours from Adelaide to Perth and stopped off to visit Bon's family. Isa met us at the airport. She drove us home as the sun went down, back to the family home in Harvest Road, on the north side of Fremantle. Bon was born in Scotland but he grew up in that port-side town, just outside of the city of Perth. It was dark when we arrived and you could see the moonlight reflected on the water. The port was full of twinkling lights where boats were moored for the evening. *How pretty*, I thought.

Bon's father, Chick, met us at the door with a big smile on his face and the craggy eyebrows of a true Scotsman.

'Welcome to the Scott clan,' he said, shaking my hand.

Chick was gentle and very sweet. He was quiet, whereas Isa

had a big voice and that lovely, tripping laugh. She never ran out of conversation. Chick broke the ice with me by telling me a terrible Dad joke.

'What's the definition of a Scottish robot?' he asked. 'Thair *boats* that ya *row*.'

Isa showed us the bedroom. She and Chick had moved into the guest room and given us their bed, which was incredibly sweet. They wanted the newlyweds to be comfortable.

The next morning, I pulled up the blinds expecting a pretty daytime version of Fremantle-by-night and found the rough, industrial landscape of a working port. *This is where Bon grew up,* I thought. It wasn't much to look at. The Scott house was small and run down, with a concrete floor in the bathroom and a Laminex table in the kitchen. It would have been cramped with Bon and his two brothers running around, but it was cosy. It felt lived in.

Bon's brother Derek came round to meet me with his wife Val and their children, Mark and Paul. They were all so lovely, especially Val. She had a beautiful little smile and she giggled a lot, and Bon giggled along with her. They had the easy rapport of two people who've known each other a long while. The whole family was relaxed and kind, and Bon was happy. I spent the morning drinking tea and listening while they talked about old friends and family.

We ate lunch on TV trays, sitting around the living room. Baby Paul was in a high chair, a cute little kid with a lid of golden girls. His brother Mark was a toddler and spent the whole day running around between our legs. They both loved Bon. Bon messed around with them, played jokes on them and made them laugh, and snuck treats out of his pocket when their Mum wasn't looking. He didn't have much practice but he made a great uncle.

In the afternoon, Bon and I walked around Fremantle, not that there was much to see. It was a grey town. The water was grey. The buildings were grey. It was a grim sort of place. We stopped at a charity shop to kill time and Bon tried on a tweed jacket that was about four sizes too big.

'What do you think, 'Rene?' he asked.

'What do you mean, what do I think?' I laughed. 'It doesn't fit you!'

As word spread that Bon was in town, his friends started to drop by. I met a guy called Ted Ward who had been in The Valentines with Bon, and the two of them reminisced about the social dances around Perth every Friday and Saturday night, and playing music to get girls.

The Fremantle Football Club had a social while we were in town, and we went along to catch up with more of Bon's friends from around the neighbourhood. There was a boring old band playing the classics and Bon leapt straight on to the dance floor, gliding the mother of an old friend around in a waltz. She was quite a solid woman, but the two of them looked like ballroom regulars. I have no idea where he learned to dance like that. Back in the Sixties they had sixty/forty dances, where the band played sixty per cent old-time music and forty per cent Bill Haley-era rock 'n' roll. Maybe Bon went to a few of those.

He gave me a wink when he came off the dance floor.

'Whaddya think of my water pumping?' he asked. It took a few seconds before I realised he meant the up-down-up-down motion of his arm, as he clasped the old woman and spun her around the floor. He wasn't fooling anyone - I knew he loved it.

We were on our way into Perth for the last day of our visit when Bon walked into the kitchen wearing his favourite purple porno T-shirt. Isa just shook her head when she saw it, as if the T-shirt had a stain on it instead of two naked women and a man having sex.

'Oh Ron,' she sighed. 'You're no wearin' that are ye?'

Bon just laughed. Isa took Bon in her stride. She and Chick were so conservative and nice, it was a mystery that he had turned out so wild. He wouldn't think twice about raiding his Mum's fridge for a beer, even when he was a teenager (or so he told me). But he must have had some inkling that the porno shirt was a bit controversial because he never wore it around my Mum. I would have died. I think Bon knew his family loved him and accepted him however he came. They knew that he was a fundamentally decent person and didn't fuss too much about the details.

In mid-June, we left Perth on a KL Airlines flight, bound for

Singapore. The minute Bon realised that the booze was free, the gloves were off. *Ding* went the bell.

'Double scotch, thanks.'

Ding, ding, ding.

'Think we'll have another!'

Ding, ding, ding, ding, ding, ding, ding. There was no in-flight entertainment back then, so the best we could do to entertain ourselves was get really drunk, pass out, then wake up and do it all over again. We had the poor air hostesses running up and down the aisles like hamsters.

We stayed in Singapore for a week; I have no idea why. We had no money for shopping and neither of us spoke Chinese, so the best we could do was wander the streets around our hotel and see what we could see. It was another world for Bon. Being surrounded by Asian people in a country so different to Australia just blew his mind. His language got really colourful.

'Fuck me, would you look at that fucking thing!'

He didn't feel uncomfortable or lost. On the contrary, he seemed to really enjoy himself. It was all just *fucking delightful*. We passed an open window one day and a very terrible version of the very terrible song 'Yellow River' came drifting out towards us. A band was rehearsing inside without much more than a couple of singers and a badly tuned guitar. Bon thought it was hilarious; he was bent over laughing. But the people of Singapore got their own back when we stopped at the street stalls to eat. Bon was hopeless with chopsticks and he spent a lot of time chasing noodles around his plate, trying hopelessly to trap the food and fling it into his mouth. The street kids would crowd round him every single time, giggling their heads off. It made Bon smile. He started playing up to it after a while.

On our way out of Singapore, the man at customs asked us to pay a departure tax, which pissed Bon off no end. He thought we were being fleeced. *Oh no*, I groaned to myself. He already stood out like a sore thumb. People generally tried to look respectable for their passport photos in the early Seventies, but not Bon. His photo looked like a Rolling Stone cover shoot. He had long hair and a bare chest, and he was pulling his best rock-star face - head tilted up with his lips slightly parted. I reckon he used to rehearse that face in front of the mirror.

When the airport official asked him to pay the tax, Bon started to get really aggravated. The guy was calm and kept smiling. Instead of being nasty, he tried to distract Bon by asking him about his tattoos.

'Mr Scott,' he said. 'Where you get this thing on your arm?'

'I was in jail,' Bon told him, 'For killing a man.'

We flew into Gatwick airport on June 21, 1972 and whipped straight through customs. Bon had a British passport and I was his wife so we didn't have to queue with the rest of the international riff-raff. *This is brilliant*, I thought. We made our way to the tube station and I was just about to walk up to the ticket counter when I remembered to ask Bon where we were going; Hamish had given him the address for the house he had rented for the band. Bon started digging around in his pockets and tossing things around in his bag.

'Ah shit,' he said.

He'd lost the piece of paper with the address written on it. He thought he might have left it in the pocket of his brown suit, which he accidentally left behind in the hotel cupboard in Singapore (we had the hotel forward it on to us later). I had this rising feeling of panic because I was so tired, but Bon managed to find another scrap of paper with Hamish's UK number on it. He had arrived in London ahead of us and was staying in a flat in Mayfair. We found some change, a red phone box ("Dr Who!" Bon grinned) and called Hamish for the address.

The tube took us to central London and then we switched to the Northern Line and rode out past Kentish Town and Highgate to Finchley Central Station. The Fraternity house was at 38 Mountfield Road in Finchley, a working-class suburb in north-west London. It was north of Golders Green, an affluent Jewish neighbourhood, and north-west of the stretch of woods at Hampstead Heath. Muswell Hill, a pretty little middle-class suburb, was over to the east. Finchley wasn't as nice as any of those areas, but it wasn't rough. It was an unremarkable kind of place with a pub on the high street and a tube station where you needed a tube station to be.

66

Bon spent the whole trip out to Finchley staring around with a huge grin on his face. I remembered exactly how it felt, being in London for the first time. Even on the tube, you got the sense that this huge city was pressing down around you, and everyone talked like they were on the telly. Bon thought it was hilarious.

When we arrived at the house we were greeted with cheers and slaps on the back; the whole crew was thrilled that another couple had made it. They were probably relieved that Bon had made it in one piece.

'The bottle shop is right on the corner!' Uncle told us.

'Better get us a drink, then,' Bon replied.

The house was a four-storey red brick with classic Sixties décor, hideous orange and yellow curtains hanging in the bay windows and floral-patterned wallpaper on the walls. The front door opened on to a narrow hallway with a set of stairs that ran up to the first floor kitchen. On the bottom floor, the nearest room had been taken over by John and Cheryl. At the end of the hallway there was a little void where one section of the house ended and another one began, with just enough space to throw a mattress. Uncle and poor Vicki (who paid her own way over) had to make do with that. On the other side of Uncle and Vicki's crawl space, in another section of the house, Mick Jurd and Carol had a room with its own sink. It doesn't sound like much, but it was a huge bonus for them in a house with a small kitchen, a single bathroom and more than a dozen tenants.

There was a lounge on the first floor with a divan under the window and beds against each of the walls. The single blokes were shunted away in there; lovely Sam See, the pianist and sometimes guitar player, Rob Booth the roadie, and Bruce King. (I have no idea what Bruce was doing with the band. He was friendly enough and always smiling. I think he once said, 'I'll get on to Hamish about that', so maybe he was supposed to be Fraternity's tour manager.) Bob Noble, the other roadie, had a room just off the second-floor landing that he shared with his partner Robyn and their baby, Jai. John Freeman and his wife Anita (Vicki's sister) had a room on the same floor; above them in the attic were Bruce Howe and Anne, his pregnant wife. (I don't know whose genius idea it was to put the heavily pregnant woman on the top floor. A few months after we arrived, she fell down the stairs and broke her leg.)

When all the backslapping was done, Bruce showed us to our room, a tiny double on the bottom floor with the Bissets on one side and Vicky and Uncle's crawlspace on the other. A set of French doors on the far side of our bedroom opened on to the back yard, which meant people had to walk through our room to hang out their washing. The walls were so thin they felt like cardboard, but we had a mattress on a proper base, which was very fancy under the circumstances. There was a small table in the corner, which became our makeshift kitchen, with a kettle and some orange, metal picnic cups next to jars of coffee and honey.

It was the middle of summer when we arrived and Bon opened up the double doors and let the light flood in. We were the last couple to arrive and we hadn't done too badly, all things considered. There were nineteen people in that house - seventeen adults, two kids and a dog - jammed into every available corner. But we had our own little space. I thought that would be enough.

The household laughed and drank its way through our first night in London, full of babbling conversation about the trip and what had been happening since the others had arrived, and what lay ahead, especially for the band. Spirits were high. With so many people in the house, we thought it would be an endless party - and who wouldn't love that? It was going to be brilliant. We were all very optimistic back then; terribly optimistic and terribly dumb.

July 10, 1972

Dear Mum and Fay,

At work on Monday. Got your letter this morning. The mail-man comes early, before the milkman. The milky brings bread, butter, eggs and everything but the proverbial kitchen sink.

It was Bon's birthday yesterday. I gave him an electric shaver and a bottle of brandy. Brandy costs double the price of home! We never go out since we can't afford it and still haven't had any pay since the Department of Civil Aviation so the old bank balance has halved. We get paid monthly in this job, about forty dollars less a fortnight than home.

Fraternity start recording in two weeks. I don't think they're too happy about it as they're not ready. The groups over here shit me to tears, with everything from eye glitter to satin trousers.

Had a card from Andrea from Singapore. She's met some Canadian guy and is going to Bali with him for a while and is coming to London for about three weeks.

It's bloody cold over here. I think they forgot to order summer this year.

Love,

Irene

We had a lovely lady next door to us on Mountfield Road who loaned us her sewing machine. There was a friendly Jamaican family up the road, a bottle shop on the corner as promised, and Finchley high street was an easy walk away. The pub at Finchley Central was nothing special but it was comfortable, and it was a nice change of scenery when we all got sick of drinking at home. I went to the high street looking for work a day or two after we landed, and found a job in the typing pool with the London Borough of Barnet. The pay was terrible. I moved over to a real estate agent's office shortly afterwards, to make a bit more money, but the boss was a slave driver and I was always working late.

The boys didn't go out looking for work because Fraternity was their job. As soon as Hamish started lining up shows for them they'd be on the road or gigging around London. Until then, it was up to the women to keep things ticking over. Bon and I never had a conversation about it, but it was understood that I was going to support him. He took it for granted and I didn't have a problem with it because I loved him and I had always worked. I just went out and did what I had always done. I suppose that in a different era, the bloke went off to work and the wife stayed at home getting her hair done and waiting for the kids to come home from school, but it didn't occur to me. You didn't expect a bloke to look after you in the Seventies, you just did what was practical. And besides, the situation with Bon and I was only temporary. Fraternity would start making money - maybe a lot of money - and then we would all benefit.

To their credit, the guys took the band very seriously. Band meetings were a big deal, especially when Hamish was due to come over. You'd hear a mutter run through the house, 'Hamish is coming, Hamish is coming.' *Clear out and let the men folk talk, ladies*.

As the rest of us found our feet over in Finchley, Hamish was trying to establish himself as a band promoter in London. He was just as bad as the guys when it came to his arrogant faith in Fraternity; he believed in the band and he was sure they would open doors for him. We gave him a bit of lip behind his back for being a privileged rich kid, but everyone respected him. I had a real soft spot for Hamish; I think his heart was in the right place. He had shipped more than a dozen people to England and set them all up in a house because he was convinced they were worth it, and that it would pay off fast. I think he was genuinely surprised when it didn't. Meanwhile, we were all very blasé about the fact that Hamish was paying the rent and utilities. We didn't give it very much thought at the time, he was just doing his part for our collective future.

August 14, 1972

Dear Mum and Fay,

Not much more news, but I had to write for something to do. Went to a party on Saturday night in our bus. There was twenty gallons of home-made booze there so I did it again! Didn't chunder though. It was a horrible party but our team soon changed that. The people there kept bopping away to The Supremes and every time we put on a record that was a bit better they'd all leave the room.

Fay, I walked from Oxford Street for miles looking for something for you but saw sweet bugger all. Typically, Irene ended up getting something for herself. Only 2 pounds! Cloggy things in brown, cheap but they're ok. I'll have to save for winter or I'll freeze my bum off.

I really miss Australia, so does Bon, but it looks like we're stuck in this dump for a while to come. Had a letter from Bon's Mum today. She's thinking of selling her house to give Bon's brother Derek and wife money for a house. Bon's really mad about it and so am I. He wrote back straight away telling her not to.

Bon was told the other day that sometime this year they will be gigging in either Germany, Jersey, Spain or England. Shit! They'll put down a single at the end of the month. It won't be the 'Tiger' one, like I thought.

(Hamish took the guys to the pub, just for sandwiches and beer, and the bloody sandwiches had maggots in them! Pommy bastards!!)

Write soon,

Love Irene

I earned what I could and so did the other girls, but right from the get-go things were tight. Fraternity went from playing eight gigs a week in Adelaide to none at all in London, so there was no income at all from the band and a lot of mouths to feed on Mountfield Road. While they waited for things to kick off with the band, the guys drank, smoked dope and played cricket in the back yard. They bought a pool table at some point, and arranged it on top of the existing table in the kitchen. There was just about enough space for it, although sometimes an arm or a cue popped out of the kitchen window to line up the perfect shot. I would come home and find the men standing around with a beer in hand, listening to The Rolling Stones and knocking their balls around, with nothing better to do. They rehearsed regularly but it wasn't practice they needed, it was a gig.

Meanwhile, the women tried to get some semblance of order happening in the house. Seventeen-year-old Anita drew up a roster for cooking and cleaning. The single guys were supposed to clean the bathroom and the toilet, and each night a different couple would make dinner for the house. (We had to get quite creative with no money and nineteen mouths to feed.) When the call came down that dinner was ready, people would shuffle up the stairs in a queue to collect their meal. It was like a soup kitchen. The couple on duty would slap food on to plates, *thwack*, then one by one the other couples would peel off to go and eat in their room. There wasn't enough space around the table for the lot of us to eat together.

You learn a lot about people in situations like that. Who was going to cook a decent feed and who was going to shove a packet of party pies in the oven? Who really gave a shit if their food was even *edible*? Mick and Carol often made this bizarre mackerel dish, which was luminous yellow. It had rice and egg, and loads of turmeric, and everyone knew they were in for a rough night when they ate it. Bon was still proudly serving his cheese coleslaw, at least until we mastered fried rice (and what a revelation that was). But some of our housemates took pride in the kitchen. Bruce taught me how to make a pasta sauce with big chunks of meat and bacon, and we all got to be expert curry chefs. (Bon loved my curries. With a little bit of guidance, my cooking skills had finally improved.)

The novelty of our titanic household wore off fast. The strain of budgeting for barn-sized meals and the lack of privacy made people tetchy. People bitched about the hot water and bitched about access to the washing machine and bitched about the constantly untidy communal areas. But mostly, people bitched about the milk - the milk situation got downright feral. Milk supplies were strictly rationed; each couple was allowed two-thirds of a pint of milk a day. Some people ate cereal and some people didn't, and inevitably there were arguments about who had had more milk than they were supposed to. People marked lines on the bottles and accused each other like they were in some bloody courtroom drama. It would have been funny if it wasn't so depressing.

Bon and I tried to stay out of it. We didn't eat cereal, and Bon just didn't like arguments. The one time I did go looking for the milk, it had disappeared into someone's bedroom.

'Hey, have you guys got the milk in there?' I called through the door.

'We have a right to our two-thirds!' they yelled back.

I decided to start drinking my coffee black.

Bon and I were content in the beginning. We were still in a bit of a newlywed bubble, even if we were living in the world's biggest share house. We stuck together and stayed out of people's way, and let the rest of them squabble over butter and bin night. I took him on adventures around London to show him all the places I knew and he was forever bouncing off the walls, full of enthusiasm. He loved to laugh at the poms and got a real kick out of imitating their accents. He was such a force of nature, I don't think the British knew what to make of him.

He went down to the local fish shop one day in his purple porno T-shirt and the worst ball-busting shorts I have ever seen. I couldn't believe he had brought them over to England. They were denim cut-offs and they were falling apart - the inner seam was so far gone it looked like he was wearing a skirt. And his balls peaked out every now and again.

'You can't wear them,' I told him. 'You just can't.'

Bon laughed and walked straight out the front door. When we got to the shop there was a queue of people waiting to buy fish, but Bon walked right past them. He strolled up to the counter and started his own queue, while the other shoppers looked on with their mouths hanging open. He got served straight away; I don't know if it was because the fishmonger admired his brazenness or because he wanted Bon's balls out of the shop.

Bon could be really crude, but he was always funny. He was terrible around women, especially in London. His eyes were all over the place. If we passed a particularly gorgeous girl, he'd turn to me with a big grin on his face and say 'Phwoar, look at that!', like I was his mate instead of his wife. In a funny way, his openness made his flirting seem very innocent, like he couldn't help himself.

We walked past a woman loading shopping into the back seat of her car who revealed the most brilliant white underwear as she bent over. Bon spun around as he passed her and growled, then turned around and kept walking along beside me as if nothing had happened. I couldn't help but laugh. He always had a thing for white cottontails.

August 23, 1972

Hi Mum and Fay,

Got your combined letters this morning. Bon's too lazy to write. He always says he'll write tomorrow but he doesn't. The bugger's only written once to his Mum so I write to her.

He played last Thursday night at Bournemouth. They went over well except their gear wasn't powerful enough, like the other groups, for the big hall.

News! Bon is off to Germany in about five weeks to do a resident's spot for about five weeks at a club called the Zoon Club. It's not all definite yet, though I'll be pissed off.

Hamish flew back to Adelaide yesterday for three weeks to fix some of his other businesses. He's got an office in Marble Arch now with orange carpet, space-age white furniture, etc. The paper clipping that Gran was talking about was sent over here by Bruce's Mum.

Fraternity are going to re-release Flaming Galah and do it all better. 'Welfare Boogie' has a different start. It starts with a guitar solo. Also has a different version of 'If You've Got It'.

I know for sure they'll make it on the continent but I'm worried about here. Poms are fickle at the moment. They're really taking to the glittery bands phase, they wear it in their hair, with satin and sequined sparkling clothes. It could affect our mob badly.

Have gone off the pill for a month and I don't like it. It's making me fat and depressed.

Love to all,

Irene

We watched the 1972 Olympic Games on a colour television. No one in the house had owned a colour television before, although I had seen one through a shop window in Adelaide. We all crowded around the set in Mountfield Road, saying 'Jesus, would you look at that.'

We learned as much about Britain watching TV as we did wandering around London. There were soaps like Coronation Street, where everyone was always down the pub, and news shows where all the presenters were complete toffs with plummy accents. Bon loved English comedy, especially Monty Python and Benny Hill, which were both on telly at the time. That was so typical of Bon - you'd get the strange, surreal humour of the Monty Python crew, which was quite intellectual, then Benny Hill chasing topless girls around for ten minutes; he'd laugh just as hard at both.

The other thing we started watching was Top of the Pops, which was on every Thursday night. Bands would come on the show and perform, miming along to their new single, and the host would count down the week's Top Ten singles. We watched The Old Grey Whistle Test as well, which was a slightly more mature version of the same thing.

We couldn't wrap our heads around the British music scene. There were all these new acts getting a run on television, like Bowie and The Sweet, Gary Glitter and Roxy Music, who to be perfectly frank seemed like a bunch of clowns. Fraternity was very much a button-down country-rock act, with their denim and their RM Williams boots. They just didn't understand glam rock. Bryan Ferry was on Top of the Pops one night, covered in sequins, and Bon and the boys absolutely killed themselves laughing.

'Come and check out this poofda!' Bon yelled at me.

The problem was that glam rock was in fashion and Fraternity wasn't.

We'd been in London over a month before the gigs started rolling in, and even then they weren't particularly impressive. Hamish had the band signed to a booking agency called MAM, but no one knew Fraternity in England so it was impossible to get decent shows. I think part of the problem was that Hamish wanted to launch them straight into the big time. The guys were playing to huge audiences back in Adelaide, so there was this expectation that they would be able to play the best clubs in London, to get really great support slots right off the bat, but it just didn't work that way. It took them a while to realise that they had to take whatever they could get.

Their first gig was at a completely nondescript pub and the audience was just the wives and a few pub locals. Fraternity played like they were back at the Largs Pier, as loudly as possible. When their first set ended, some crappy Top 40 pop music came on over the speakers and a topless dancer began gyrating half-heartedly around the floor, one eye on the clock. She disappeared back into the kitchen afterwards. She probably went to do the dishes.

They played at the Speakeasy Club in Soho a couple of weeks later. It was an important gig at a very cool venue that had hosted everyone from Jimi Hendrix to Hawkwind, but Fraternity didn't leave a mark on the place. They had issues with their gear, which was out of date, and there was no audience to fuel their performance. They just didn't fire - not the way they had back home.

Hamish started booking them out of town. He had had the old Greyhound bus shipped over from Australia and the band took it on the road whenever they picked up a support slot, which started happening here and there. In Bournemouth, the guys supported Status Quo, who had had a minor hit in the late Sixties with 'Pictures of Matchstick Men'. Fraternity didn't know anything about them; they certainly didn't know that Status Quo were about to become one of the world's biggest rock bands. All Fraternity knew was that Status Quo arrived in Bentleys, wearing flash Savile Row outfits, and changed into their jeans and T-shirts for the show. The Fraternity guys were in fits of laughter; they were convinced they'd blow the headline act off the stage. But they were wrong. Status Quo were twice as loud and twice as good as Fraternity, according to Sam See. The guys played it down, but they were obviously quite deflated.

The planned re-release of Flaming Galah didn't happen. They talked about recording a new album, but that didn't happen either. They were constantly scheming to kick-start their career in Europe, but for some reason the plan was always changing. Us girls just left them to it. We figured that the guys would figure it out. In the meantime, I gave my Mum and sister all the good news I could scrape together.

September 6, 1972

Dear Mum and Fay,

I hope the money and present arrived ok. The money, in case you didn't get my last letter, is for some bras from John Martins. It's too far to go into the city out here, and besides they don't sell them. Also every time I go in with money, I spend it and come home with nothing.

Bon played last Friday night at the Speakeasy, which is a nightclub that musicians go to when they've finished playing. The Kinks were sitting at the bar, also Chris Farlowe asked who the group was. I flaked out in the bus and only heard them do the last number. They played at 2am and I was out at 11pm and didn't come around 'til 3am. I'd only had two brandys but I'm not used to spirits anymore as we can't afford them. A London bobby helped me out of the window of the bus when he saw that I couldn't get out.

It's bloody freezing here today but was really hot two days ago. Mad place. Bon and me made a really nice fried rice dish for everyone. Bacon from the butchers, 6lb, fried separately, then add 1 dozen eggs, fried separately and chopped up. Boil rice and then fry it with capsicum, shallots, celery, onions, peas - yum! It's bloody hard cooking for eighteen. I really miss chops to have one for me. I haven't had one since home.

Bon's Mum can't cook for nuts. His idea of a roast is to eat the meat when it's warm with a few roast potatoes that usually cook when the meat is taken out. No gravy, that's all. Weird Scots.

Anne's baby is due two days before my birthday. I told Bon that he'll have to start sneaking a few more pence out of my purse to give me a present.

Love,

Irene

PS. Andrea rang last week and said she was coming round that night but she didn't, and she's away somewhere again.

78

Andrea made her way to London in August but she only stayed for a night. She managed to make it pretty memorable. Before we'd left Adelaide, she had invited Bon and I round for a farewell dinner. She was headed to Western Australia to work in the mines and we were off to the UK, so it was last drinks for all of us for a while. When Bon and I started dating, Andrea had left us to it, but she was very affectionate towards Bon over dinner and it made me feel a bit odd.

By the time she landed in London, Andrea was a little more straightforward. She flirted with Bon like crazy. On the way back from the pub she said, 'Your husband's got a really nice bum', then she bent over and bit him on the arse.

Bon jumped about a foot in the air. I would have punched Andrea but she was a lot stronger than me. And besides, I couldn't really blame her.

Everyone liked Bon. He was a bit of a lunatic, but he had a beautiful nature and he usually did the right thing. If we were on the high street and someone was out collecting for the Salvos, for example, Bon was always the first to drop a few spare coins in the tin.

'Paying my insurance,' he'd wink.

He made the same joke every time.

Bon was a people person and he was surrounded constantly in Mountfield Road. In a strange way, in the beginning at least, it was probably one of the happiest times of his life. The party lasted a lot longer for him than it did for me. He had his mates, plenty of beer, a bit of dope, and the occasional bit of something else if the day wasn't moving fast enough.

I came home from work one evening and found him spaced out on the floor of the bedroom, giggling to himself as he picked at the carpet. I sighed as I dropped the shopping on the table, and shouted into the hallway.

'Anyone know what's happened to Bon?'

Vicki told me he'd eaten datura, a hallucinogenic plant. He seemed happy enough, but he was right off the planet and didn't look like he was coming down soon. I made

Uncle call the guy who sold it to Bon and ask him what we should do. The dealer said we should make Bon drink lemon juice. It was the closest thing we had to an expert medical opinion, so we flooded the poor bastard with it until he started to throw up.

When he wasn't experimenting with the local plant life, Bon was usually buried in his notebook. Even though plans to record had been shelved, he was always working on new lyrics. He would think up these jokey one-liners and scribble them down, then build ideas for songs around them. A lot of them made me laugh, but sometimes I was just puzzled.

'Women like you are rare as rocking-horse shit,' he read.
'What the hell is rocking-horse shit?' I laughed.

'Rare as rocking-horse shit' was an ocker expression but I'd never heard it before. It was Bon's toilet poetry, weaving its way into his songwriting.

He liked to be controversial, and if he could mix a bit of controversy with a good laugh, he was happy - that's how I got him in drag. We were sitting around bored on a Saturday night when I suggested he try on some of my clothes.

'I'll make you very pretty,' I promised him.
'Yeah, alright,' he laughed.

I put a ton of make-up on him, black eyeliner and burgundy lipstick, and squeezed him into black tights, a pair of my shorts and a velvet jacket, with a strappy pair of heels and a handbag to finish him off. He looked like a really ugly drag queen. He tottered up the stairs and into the lounge room, where a shocked silence was followed by roaring laughter.

'Jesus,' shouted one of the guys, 'I nearly cracked a fat.'

September, 1972

Dear Mum and Faye,

There were big dramas at the house yesterday. The Cheryl and John situation has been upsetting the group ever since John joined. Mick was so fed up that he said either John goes or he does. Mick refused to play with the band again until it was settled. Everyone was really upset but we all hate Cheryl, so it looked like John was getting his marching orders.

Hamish is in Sydney. He was located and phoned at 2am this morning. He talked to Mick and told him it would be the finish of Fraternity if he left, and told him that he had the job of keeping the band together. John has to stay and Cheryl is to get out. The company is paying for her to go into a flat, which makes me mad because once again she is using it to get what she wants. But Brent is a thorough bastard and I'll be glad to see the last of him.

Bon is playing at the Speakeasy again on Saturday night. Had a letter from Bon's Mum today. She can't sell the house because no one wants it.

I drew out money for a dressing gown and got a warm one. I wanted one like Mum's but couldn't get one. Went off the pill for a month and was shitting myself up 'til today in case I copped a bun in the oven. If we get rich I might give it a second thought. Don't write back like I've said anything or Bon will have a fit.

We're still as happy as anything so don't worry, Ma.

Love,

Irene (and Bon)

Cheryl and John fought like cats and dogs, even before we left Adelaide. London only made things worse; the two of them were at each other's throats. No one was particularly upset that Cheryl wanted to move out, but it was bad news for the band. Things weren't coming together the way they expected and everyone was broke. The strain was starting to affect everyone.

Hamish managed to get Fraternity a few more support slots in London and a few more out-of-town shows. They played with Atomic Rooster, whose single 'Tomorrow Night' had gone Top 20 in the UK the previous year. They supported Fairport Convention, who were big at the time, and a psychedelic rock band from London called Pink Fairies.

When the band got booked for a gig in Cambridge, we all piled into the Greyhound, just for a change of scenery. Poor old Rob had lots of trouble trying to negotiate the tiny, cobbled streets in a 40-seater bus. The same thing happened when we went up to Liverpool; Rob scraped past buildings and pumped the air brakes to get us around corners in a fifteen-point turn.

It wasn't just the bus; the band's gear was oversized as well. They were booked to play The Cavern in Liverpool but their gear was too big to fit on the stage - not that that was going to stop them from playing. We'd seen pictures of all the great Merseyside bands playing at The Cavern, The Beatles particularly, and we were really awestruck by the place, no matter how grimy and dark it was. The ground floor had sticky black linoleum that clung to your shoes and the ladies' toilet had recently deposited vomit in the hand basin, but it was a part of music history! It was disgusting, but it was legendary.

We slept in a boarding house that night, on sheets that looked like they hadn't been changed since the mid-Fifties. The mattresses sat on wire frames that sagged so low they scraped the floor and the walls looked like they were about to collapse. It was the kind of place you'd only stay if you were a struggling musician - in fact they seemed to be the only clientele. The landlady had pictures on the wall of all the noteworthy musicians that had been her guests, going all the way back to Tommy Steele.

'You should put our picture up there,' Bon winked.

I was always worried about money, but as winter came on and we struggled with something as basic as keeping warm, the situation got a little ridiculous. I couldn't help but think, *if Bon just got a job...* but it wasn't on the cards. It occurred to me at some point that Hamish hadn't brought the wives over to London out of generosity, he'd done it out of necessity. He needed us to take care of the men because it took the pressure off of him.

As the year wore on and everyone's nerves started to fray, the band meetings with Hamish became more and more irritating. It irked the women to be banished from the room while the men talked important business when the women were the ones keeping everything afloat. It was like a bad joke. Bon was frustrated with their lack of progress, but it didn't make him appreciate me any better. He'd just wave me out of the way when it was time to talk business, like the coffee lady getting shooed out of the boardroom. That was the real irony. We got just enough of the sexual revolution to let us go out and get jobs, but the guys didn't really see us as equal partners, working towards the same goal. Our lives revolved around them, and for some reason we just accepted it.

September 18, 1972

Dear Fay,

It's getting colder and colder and rainier here by the day. Bought a heater today for £3 and we're getting a warm blanket (£7) on hire purchase. I really need jumpers as my black one's thin and I've only a polo neck. Might get one this pay.

Fraternity played at the Speakeasy again on Saturday night and really went down well. The bad news - to me that is - is that they're supposed to be off to Europe for five weeks next month and may be in Switzerland for Christmas, in some chalet in the Alps. Which means that I haven't exactly got much of a future to look forward to.

They only play at good jobs, which is why they haven't worked much. It's something to do with a sort of air about them being a good group, which the agency is building around them. They could do dozens of shit jobs if they wanted to.

I'll be really lonely when they go because the house shits me, there's nothing to do. The girls are not really great friends of mine. I don't know what I'll do. What a Christmas.

I'm thinking that tax check isn't coming at all? I wanted to blow it on some warm stuff for Bon and me. I walked my bloody feet off today trying to find the heater!

No little nephew accidents, thank Christ. It would have starved anyway.

I went to see Max Merritt on Friday at the Speakeasy and they were shithouse - an embarrassment to Oz. I hear Australia has forgotten Fraternity pretty well.

Give my love to Mum,

Irene

PS. Bon's had some bloke perving on his bum, reading the brand name. 'Ooooo, slim fits! And they certainly are slim fits, aren't they, duckie?' !!!

September 26, 1972

Dear Mum and Fay,

Got the cheque the other day, thanks! First thing I bought with it was a bottle of brandy for Bon. He never drinks it over here as it's very expensive. I couldn't find what I wanted and got confused, and ended up buying just a jumper. I needed it anyway. London is so huge and crowded it's impossible to shop.

Had a letter from Andrea the other day from Amsterdam. She's gone right off her brain. I knew travelling would do it to her. She doesn't want to write anymore as she is 'too different' from me now and I just 'wouldn't understand'. She's been mixing with too many nutty Americans.

Bon goes away to Europe next month for five weeks. The longer I stay in this place the more I wish we could get back to Australia, but I guess that day is a long way off. No one likes it here, Fay.

Bon had a letter from his fan club president in Sydney today. She reckons everyone's really forgotten about Fraternity. We'll have the last laugh one day. Remember how big and loud their gear was in Australia? It used to shit over other groups. Well it's nothing over here but they're getting new stuff, so imagine how great they'll sound when/if they one day go back?

Love,

Irene

October 2, 1972

Dear Mum,

I've been pretty worried since Fay said she was getting married. I can't help but think she's only doing it to get herself out of a rut because she sounded so fed up and miserable. I don't know what to think. It seems that she's just doing something drastic. I certainly hope I'm wrong because I'd hate her to be miserable for the rest of her life.

I can hardly preach because I haven't been married that long, but Bon was exactly what I wanted. I think he's fantastic and he's really good to me. I have him running around like a mother hen sometimes.

If everything's ok and she's really sure then I'll just be shitty 'cause I can't be there. She's welcome to my dress. I'd be more than pleased if she wants to borrow it, but I guess she'll want something new. Have you got enough money, Mum? If you want I'll send some towards it. She'll have to wait 'til I can get something one day for a present.

I think it's really lousy that I have to miss out on this. Why don't you economise for the reception and maybe have it at home? I'm worrying that maybe the big hole I blew in your bank book [for my wedding] won't allow much for Fay so I don't mind giving what I can.

If I was at home earning good money I'd go you halves, but I'm afraid I'm living like the proverbial pauper over here. My feet are bad again from wearing my high boots but it's too cold to wear shoes unless you've got thick tights. I might have to get some flat-heeled boots but I begrudge paying the £12.

Lots of love,

Irene

Bon wasn't a bad bloke. I don't think he felt like he was doing anything wrong in asking me to support him while they tried to get Fraternity off the ground. I think he just had it in his head that they would get to a point where they were successful and then he would take care of me. In the meantime, he could be really kind. He always helped with the washing, or asked if I was warm enough, or asked if I wanted a cup of coffee. And he was generous when he had money; he just didn't have much of it back then.

Bon bought me earrings for my 22nd birthday, or so he told me. He said they'd fallen out of his pocket when we were out playing pool. I was heartbroken; I really thought he was joking. On the way to work the next day, I stopped to look in the window of a little antique shop, at a 19th-century beaded purse that I loved. I'd been coveting it for a while and had dropped a few hints to Bon, thinking maybe he'd get the idea. To make matters worse after my disappointing birthday, there was an empty space where the purse used to sit and the shopkeeper told me it was sold. When I got home from work that day, miserable and self-pitying, Bon presented me with a box.

'Cheer up, 'Rene,' he smiled, and gave me a kiss.

The little beaded purse was inside.

CHAPTER 5

GRUSS AUS GOSLAR/HARZ

p/m 2.11.72

Mrs Thornton & Daughter

6 York St Propect S.A. Australia

Dear Mum & Faye,

This is the first town we are playing in on our 6 week tour of the continent. We'll be in Germany for the first two weeks, then a couple of weeks in France + Belgium then back to Germany. The country is beautiful & the people very friendly. Unfortunately Irene has had to stay in England (she's made me wear a chastity belt).

Have a good Xmas & New Year.

Love,
Bon x

The boys went off to Germany in November 1972 and froze their balls off. It sounded pretty positive at first; they would be supporting The Sweet and they'd get free accommodation and £145 a week for the tour. Somehow it all fell apart. They had almost no money, they were really hungry, and their accommodation was miserable. There's a picture of Bon in Germany, sitting on the bus with his hand under his chin and a dark look in his eyes. I knew it well. It's the look he got when he was pissed and dismal, and wanted to withdraw from the world. When we first got married it was pretty rare, but it got more and more familiar to me as the year went on.

Back in England, I was terribly lonely and terribly bloody cold. It started snowing early that year. With no money coming in from the tour, I took a second job in the evenings, working five nights a week as an usherette at a movie theatre. *Pretty leg-aching stuff,* I wrote to Fay, *but it will pay an extra £5 a week!* I had become really obsessed with money, which is what happens when you don't have any. (My grandmother sent me an Australian dollar bill and I swapped it at work for 50 pence - 10 shillings more than it was worth. I thought I'd won the lottery.) I also learned to take really good care of my things. The blanket we bought on hire purchase was purple wool with a purple satin trim, and Bon was shocked to see it in my room several years later.

'Don't you ever change the bed?' he laughed.

By the time the band left for Germany, the Bissets had moved into a four-bedroom cottage up the road, although John was still playing with the band. I had my eye on their old room, but Hamish decided he was going to spend £200 sound-proofing it so that Fraternity could use it as a rehearsal space. It was a bit pointless as the band was starting to fall apart. Sam See had had enough and he was on his way out. He left London in December and flew to Canada to re-join his old band, Flying Circus. John Bisset would leave in the new year to join Mungo Jerry briefly.

I spent my twenty-third birthday down at the pub with the other girls, but I missed Bon. I missed the emotional support and warmth, and the intimacy you have with someone when you talk to them and laugh with them late at night, when it's just the two of you. The other girls were feeling the same way. We were all trying to make the best of a shitty situation.

The guys made it back just in time for Christmas and said nothing about the shows. Vicki felt so bad for them that she cooked them a big turkey. Anne took a photo of Bon and I, trying to make the best of it. I'm sitting next to him in a bright pink dressing gown, which was the warmest thing I owned, and he's slumped beside me with his cap pulled low and a couple of streamers dangling limply around him. It was an absolutely miserable Christmas.

Sometime early in the new year, the guys decided that they needed a change. I think the message had finally gotten through to them that their country-rock style was off the boil and glam was really cool. Maybe they were just desperate, I don't know.

They started to make a few subtle modifications. Bruce, who

never wore anything but black T-shirts and bell-bottom jeans, had Anne sew sequins on to the back of his old denim jacket. Bon, always slightly off the mark, borrowed the silver bangles that I had bought in Bangkok and hung them in his earring. I don't know what he was going for but he looked like a pirate.

The band also changed its name from Fraternity to Fang. Their sound didn't really change at all, but I think they decided that Fang sounded a bit more glam than Fraternity. It didn't last long. They played a couple of gigs as Fang - including one with a Scottish band called Geordie, fronted by Brian Johnson - and suddenly they were Fraternity again.

April, 1973

Dear Mum and Fay,

It was good to hear from you. What records do they still play on the radio? What colour is the new lino?

Started my new job yesterday. It's really good - at last! - and in lovely surroundings. They have three goldfish tanks with coloured lights and bubbling water. One's got little turtles in it. They let me go half an hour early tonight.

I'm working for three people again and they're really nice, and not whip-crackers. One owns an E-Type Jag sports - $$$!

I've decided to let Bon handle the money from now on. This week's been pretty disastrous but he's been so much happier for it that I'm glad. Hamish said the other night there's a chance we could be going to Germany to live around August, but it depends on a lot. I better take a crash course [in German].

Bon's brother should be over next week some time. I hope he brings over some duty-free booze! I'm cooking tea and using the electric frying pan in the bedroom. You oughta get one, Mum.

Lots of love,

Irene and Bon

I found a job in a property development office, working for two very nice men, one Jewish and one English. They were very well off and I was awed by their wealth. While Bon and I scraped and pinched every penny, my bosses chatted casually about the new Rolls- Royces and Jaguars. It blew my mind.

When Bon and I fought, it was always about money. It was shitty being broke, never having enough to eat, never going out anywhere nice, being stuck in the house with a heap of other broke and miserable people. It gnawed away at the relationship. I decided to let Bon handle our money because he had none of his own and it was making him crabby. Even if there wasn't much to go around, at least he got to control the little we had. And whatever mistakes were made with money, at least he was responsible for it. I think I had enough on my plate.

With Fraternity, we faced these constant shifting sands. Plans changed every week and they got more desperate all the time; I learned not to invest too much in any of it. It was harder on Bon, because he was stuck in the house with no job and no real direction. He lit up when his brother Graeme came to visit. Graeme was always pretty cashed up and he took Bon out to quite a few gigs when he was in town. They saw The Rolling Stones, Alex Harvey and Deep Purple in London. Graeme took him to see Little Richard too, which was a shocking experience for Bon.

'He's a poof!' he told me, eyes wide.

It's strange hearing that word now, but it was a different time. I mean, fancy us not realising beforehand that Little Richard was gay.

May 20, 1973

Dear Mum,

Thought I'd write again in case you were lonely. We've definitely got the arse from our house. Hamish is looking at another one today. They're hard to find.

Had a letter from Fay today. If Kathy is still alive, tell her to write. Had a sort of a letter from Peter a few weeks back.

Hope things are going ok for you, Mum. Wish I could come back and start being a nice sort of a daughter for a change instead of the grumpy bitch I was before I met Bon. I'm still a grump to him now. He's a good little thing.

LATER: The house Hamish looked at was a dump, so back to square one. Guess what? Big thrills. I'm not going to Spain or Germany (because I'll be flat broke by August) but to Cornwall with the girls, staying at a beautiful beach in a guesthouse.

Lots of love,

Irene and Bon

In the end, most of the girls found a way to get along. Bruce's wife Anne was wise, warm and wonderful. If Bruce was like the father figure, Anne was like the mother hen; everybody felt like they could talk to her. Anita became quite close to Anne and helped her with baby Jonathan after he was born. Vicky and I became really good friends. She had a really hard time in the house, living in that walkway with Uncle, and it had a devastating effect on her. I really felt for her. As a group we didn't have a lot in common, but the misery of Mountfield Road brought us together.

The girls started a holiday fund early in 1973, stashing spare cash in a tin whenever we could. We needed a break. The guys had been away on tour, but the rest of us had been staring at the same bloody wallpaper for nearly a year. We planned a trip to the beach in Cornwall and we got very close, but at the last minute the men swooped in and appropriated the funds. The band needed the money to buy new gear.

June 6, 1973

The Thornton Girls

16 York St Prospect Adelaide, South Australia 5082

From: 38 Mountfield Rd Finchley N3 England

Dear Mum & Sis,

G'day there. How'd ya be. Well & in fine spirits I trust. We start our second tour tonight, this time with a London band, the "Pink Fairies", who are reputed to be the wildest thing this side of history. So it looks like we're in for a good time. The AMON DÜÜL (the German band) tour wasn't too bad & we got a few more jobs on the strength of our performances, though only one or two of them were in the good to very good category. Anyway it really helped us to tighten the band up and we've since played a few dates which have been really well received.

Don't know if Irene's told you but our landlord has told us we have to get out, but I'm afraid he doesn't know us Aussies when it comes to being stubborn.

Brother Graeme has been here for a few weeks now, giving all the girls in the house a change of scenery (a welcome one they'd say), & at the moment he's in Germany. He went to France last week to check out the Aust protestors on the atom bomb scene. The bugger rang me up at 7.30 this morning to get me to send him a tenner for his fare back. He's as mad as his brother.

Well I guess 'Rene would have told you anything I haven't so I'll muck off and make meself a cup of beer. Give my regards to the rest of the family and friends and I'll see you later.

Love,
Bon X

June 6, 1973

Dear Mum,

I see Bon has written you a letter so I'll post it with this. Graeme is in Germany at the moment but coming back tomorrow.

You may have one member of the Scott family staying with you next summer - Bon. Hamish went to Adelaide last night on business and is planning for the guys only to go back for a few weeks' work. I don't know how I feel about that. I thought, 'Then I'll get to Australia!' Maybe the government can pay my fare back.

You can only be mucked around so much and then you get fed up, which I am, of supporting someone for eighteen months and getting nothing in return except more shit thrown at you. I still love Bon but it won't make any difference if I have to put up with this penny-pinching existence.

Bon lost his sleeper earring last night. He had three of my silver bracelets on it and lost them too, where he played.

Wish I had a rich relation that would give me a return fare home. Can't remember if I told you that Graeme is selling me this beautiful Afghan coat that he bought at a sale for 14 quid, for only £7. It's lovely.

Bon has got off his arse to start a cleaning job next week that will pay his booze money for when he's playing during the week. He's on another tour with a group called the Pink Fairies, who aren't like what they sound.

It's Bon's birthday on July the 9th. He needs T-shirts and undies, in case you want to send anything. If you send sea mail or second-class airmail it's cheaper.

Love,
Irene

94

By mid-1973, the landlord had decided not to renew our lease at Mountfield Road, possibly because he realised that there were ten-thousand people living there. I think the garbage gave us away. There were piles of rubbish down the side of the house, which the council refused to handle. Uncle begged the garbage men to get rid of it.

'If I throw it on the truck, will you just take it away?'

'Sorry mate,' they told him. 'It's more than the job is worth.'

Hamish tried to reason with the landlord, but he wouldn't have a bar of it. We were told to be out in a month. The pressure was too much and politics in the house got really out of control all of a sudden. Rob Booth moved into the Greyhound bus and ran an extension cord up into the house; he said he wanted some peace and quiet. Mick walked into the lounge room one day with his eyes bulging out, screaming at Vicki, Anne, Anita and me. Someone had used his wife's frying pan and he went off his nut.

'My wife isn't like the rest of you molls!' Mick bellowed.

We all looked round at each other, wondering who the molls were supposed to be. *Who, us?* It was quite a shock. The mask had slipped, and someone we thought of as a friend had suddenly revealed their true feelings. We couldn't come back from something like that. We could make peace and pretend it didn't happen, but we really couldn't forget it.

June 14, 1973

Dear Mum and Fay,

The weather is sunny and warm quite often but it doesn't stay that way for long. Bon is working half days doing labour jobs, but I'm lucky if I see it. He spends it on food and booze for himself. Still, it cheers him up.

The band is doing ok but it's a long, hard struggle. Had some bad news - Bon had his ears tested and they're about the equivalent of a sixty-year-old man's. If he goes on playing in the group he'll be stone deaf in three years. It won't stop him though.

Bruce could have meningitis. He's going to have a proper test in hospital, and if he does he'll have to give up playing.

I'm thinking of buying a sewing machine as the second-hand one we got is a dud. At least when we're not completely broke I might be able to buy material and make myself some clothes.

This Sunday all us girls are doing this waitressing job for my boss. My job is really great. Not an awful lot of shorthand. I answer the switchboard ok now and have made lots of coffee.

Lot of love,

Irene

PS. Bon's birthday, July the 9th, age 27.

96

On board the Fraternity tour bus on our way
to the registry office, 24 January 1972.

Wedding guests waiting outside the registry office at Adelaide Town Hall.

Inside the registry office. My Auntie Nell is in the foreground scratching her head with my grandmother next to her, then Bon's mother, Isa, and Bruce Howe's mother on the end.

Exchanging the rings, with
Bruce Howe standing on the left
and John Bisset on the right.

As we left the registry office Bon said, 'Give us a kiss for the camera.'

A quick photo after the wedding, standing by
the back fence at Bon's place in Norwood. (L-R)
Me, Isa, Bon and Mum.

Bon's shirtless passport photo, with his trademark rock star pose, earned him a few disapproving stares from airport officials in Singapore in 1972.

Young and happy, sitting on the stairs at
Mountfield Rd.

Fraternity on the road in Germany, November
1972. A familiar dark look from Bon.

Bon standing in our
bedroom doorway at
Mountfield Road, in the
English summer of 1973.

Graeme Scott sitting on the bonnet of my FB Holden, September 1974.

Bon and me at Bob Noble's partner Robyn's 21st birthday, winter 1974 in Adelaide, after Bon's bike accident. He's wearing my father's torn airforce jacket.

A kilted Bon at AC/DC's Festival Hall gig, 31 December 1974.

Left: My 21st birthday
at the Hotel Enfield in
Adelaide, December
1971. (L–R) Fay, Mum,
Kathleen, me and Bon.

Me with tourists in 2003 at Bon's grave in Western Australia.

My boss asked if Fraternity would play a traditional Jewish function he was hosting. God knows why. Vicki and I donned aprons to serve food and Fraternity played with their usual gusto. My poor boss kept complaining about the volume and asking if they could tone it down. After the set, the guys helped themselves to the free alcohol and got roaring drunk. It was a rare happy night, though. The guys piled into the kitchen at the end of the party to help us with the dishes, crashing knives and forks around the sink while the lot of them sang Beatles tunes at the top of their lungs. I was wondering if I was still going to have a job the next day, but my boss was absolutely fine about it. He gave us jars of coffee and leftover food to take home. That was the closest Bon would get to a birthday party that year because we were too broke to throw one ourselves, but it was nothing to complain about.

July 20, 1973

Dear Ma,

Got a letter from you and from Fay a few days ago. Only a few more weeks to go 'til our Cornwall holiday and it's been raining and cold for two weeks.

The guys got a bad write-up in a paper called Melody Maker, which goes practically all over the world, for a concert they did with Mungo Jerry. It was an outdoor thing and all the sound went up in the air. Poor buggers.

Bon started his day job two days ago driving a forklift in a factory, so things should look a bit better money-wise. Hamish is going to buy a house and we'll all have to pay him rent, when he can find a place big enough.

Work told me I was in for a rise a month ago but I never got it. They got a colour telly here the other day. Boy, are they rich!

I'll send another photo of me and Bon so you can both have one.

Lots of love,

Irene

My letters home were still upbeat, but things with Bon and I were on a steady decline. Relationships are funny that way. It's hard to say exactly when things tip over from mostly happy to mostly shit, but if it hadn't happened by mid-year it wasn't far off.

Meanwhile, Hamish had given up. Fraternity had spent a year trying to break into the UK music scene and Hamish had spent god knows how much money underwriting them, and by August it was obvious to everyone that they had failed. The Melody Maker review was the last straw; there was no way the band was coming back from that. England just wasn't interested in Fraternity. The night that Hamish broke the news, everyone was really down and half the girls disappeared into their rooms to cry. Bon didn't say much about it, but his mood was black.

The last big plan that was hatched by the band was to try their luck in a different scene. Someone suggested Canada. They should have gone to North America in the first place, where prog rock and country was still popular. Maybe if they started over, they'd have a chance? The minute Bon mentioned it to me, I felt exhausted.

'I don't want to go to Canada,' I told him. 'I want to go home.'

'I've got to go with the band, 'Rene,' Bon replied.

I didn't have much of a choice. If I wanted to be with Bon, I'd have to follow him, wherever he decided to go.

August 30, 1973

Dear Mum,

Sorry I'm slow with letters but there's never anything much to tell. Still haven't found a place to live.

No one's at work today so I'm watching the telly. I couldn't get used to a black and white one now. You'd love it, Mum.

We went for our Canada interview today. They're being real bastards at work since I told them I might be going. Honesty doesn't seem to be the best policy any more, does it?

Bon wore his suit to the interview today, for the first time since Singapore. Dragged out his shirt too, which hadn't been washed since then. Boy, what a smell!

He's pretty short-tempered, you know. It's either put up with it or leave, but it gets on my nerves sometimes.

Has Fay managed to sell Bon's clock or anything? I might send my electrical stuff home as I wouldn't get much for it and you can't use it in Canada as it's completely different and can't be converted.

Speak to J.C. about us getting a flat. We'll need the odd prayer.

Sure miss you, Ma. Look after yourself.

Love,

Irene

Bon and I were killing each other. I think the pressure of things going so badly with the band created a massive wedge between us, and there was a point when we decided to just call it quits. He would go to Canada and I would go home. There wasn't much of a discussion about it. *Well that didn't work out, see ya later*, simple as that. I was heartbroken. The thought of going back to Adelaide on my own was horrible. It was like going back to square one, like our whole relationship hadn't ever happened. I was depressed but really ashamed as well - the embarrassment was almost more than I could bear. But he didn't leave and we didn't break up. Things were still shifting and changing every few days, and at some point (without much more discussion) the whole Canadian plan was shelved. The band would stay in London and we would all work until we could save enough money to get ourselves home.

Bon picked up odd jobs here and there, including working in a wig-making factory, but they never seemed to stick. I took a second job in the evenings, at the Midas Arts metal-casting workshop. Bon and I still shared a bed, and I still shared my pay check, but I didn't know what it meant anymore.

As long as we were all staying in London, we still needed somewhere to live, and the landlord still wanted us out. I found a two-bedroom flat and those of us that were left moved out of Mountfield Road - Anita and John Freeman, Bruce and Anne, Vicki and Uncle, Bon and me. We squeezed ourselves into a flat just a few blocks north of where Bon and I shared a room with Bruce, Anne and the baby. The only way I got any sleep at night was by wearing earplugs. Mercifully, it didn't last long; we were busted by the new landlord, who thought he had let his place to two nice Australian girls. He came over one evening to find almost a dozen people, packed to the rafters. Enraged, he tried to pick a fight with Uncle. Uncle, who had just arrived home on his motorcycle, elected to keep his helmet on until the landlord was ready to leave.

We moved back to Mountfield Road, but we still had an eviction notice hanging over our heads. The only hope we had was to throw ourselves on the mercy of the court. I don't know how a British judge was convinced to take pity on a bunch of Australians, but it was mostly down to Anne and the baby. Jonathan was barely six months old - he couldn't end up on the streets. Anne told the judge we were saving to go home, and he ordered the owner of Mount-field Road to let us stay until we left the country. By that stage, his house was virtually a squat.

Late in 1973, Bon finally found a job that he enjoyed (at least enough to keep doing it for more than a week). He started working as a bartender at the Manor Cottage, a pub on the corner of East End Road and the North Circular, and he was a natural. He pulled his hair back in a half ponytail and got stuck into it, pulling beer and popping lids, slinging packets of crisps over his head like an absolute pro. The locals loved him. He told them jokes and gave them a fair dose of shit and played the Aussie larrikin role to the hilt. And when his fan club got drunk enough, he taught them the words to 'Waltz-ing Matilda' and led the whole pub in a sing-a-long. Bon always did well with an audience.

We spent our last Christmas in London at the Manor Cottage, with a big old English ham and a turkey, loads of booze and laughter all around. It was a lovely day; a little oasis in a sea of shit. It was one of the last times Bon and I were really happy together.

Just after Christmas in 1973, the battered remains of the Mount-field Road household prepared to go home. We were all so relieved to be leaving and Australia was all we could talk about.

'Won't it be great to have a barbecue?'

'Won't it be great to have a cold beer in a pub back home?'

'Won't it be great to play the Pier again?'

It was the happiest we'd all been for a year.

The guys had a plan to make a bit of money, so we wouldn't go home empty-handed. They asked all the women to put in some cash to buy state-of-the-art music equipment. The plan was to sell it back home and split the profit.

'You're gonna have to empty some shit out of that trunk, Irene,' Bruce told me.

I was packing the same trunk that Hamish had given us with the things I brought with me and the few precious things I had bought, but the guys made me take a lot of it out again. I left my wedding shoes on the floor at Mountfield Road so that Bruce could cram a speaker into the trunk. I don't know if they ended up selling the gear. I didn't see a dime.

CHAPTER 6

The eighteen months that Bon and I were away passed so slowly. It was this painful downward spiral, like watching a car accident in very slow motion; everything was constantly on the verge of falling apart and we just didn't have the maturity to deal with it. We had never talked about the future or where we were headed, we'd just assumed everything would work out and we'd be well off and that would be it. We had no plan for the tough times. But England was like a rubber band, stretching us until we frayed and eventually snapped.

The worst part was feeling like I cared more than he did. I was upset about the breakdown of our marriage, but Bon was probably just as focused on the breakdown of his career. If anything, he was bewildered that I was no longer this lovely young girl with a great sense of humour. My feelings were just a pain in the arse. Towards the end, we had an argument and I ended up down at the pub by myself, wallowing in utter despair. Our relationship was hopeless; the situation was hopeless. Bon came into the pub to try and talk some sense into me, with all the sensitivity of a cricket bat.

'Why do you have to be such a downer?' he asked. 'You've got a husband that digs ya, isn't that enough?'

He wasn't a bastard. He didn't want to hurt me, he just wanted me to be the nice girl who never complained, the way he never complained. The girl that didn't fight over the milk and waited until everyone else had had their shower and worked two jobs to make ends meet. I couldn't be that girl anymore.

In the end, Fraternity had to deal with the reality that whatever people had thought of the band in Adelaide, there were plenty of other groups out there that were just as good or better than them; that maybe they weren't world class. All that egotism and self-confidence came crashing down in a heap. And Bon, who had been trying to make it for so long as a musician, was probably starting to think that it'd never happen. The death of his marriage was a really small thing compared to the death of his rock 'n' roll dreams. That's what he thought about, never our relationship. Our relationship kicked on because it was easier to keep going than to think very hard about ending it.

Nothing was ever really resolved, but by the time we left England things had mended between us, superficially at least. We just couldn't wait to leave. Between my two jobs and Bon's work at the bar, we managed to scrimp a fair bit together, but in the end we had to ask Graeme for help. He loaned us the money for our flights home. There was no spare cash for a last-minute trip to Paris or anywhere else for that matter, we just counted down the days until we left. *Please let us get to the airport, please let us get on the plane, please let us take off.* The closer we got to Australia, the lighter the atmosphere between us became.

We flew back into Perth the day before New Year's Eve and stayed with Isa and Chick in their new house. They had sold the family home to give Derek and Val a leg up, and moved into a semi-detached in Scarborough. Isa didn't love the place, but Chick had 'got off his bum and put a garden in', which according to Bon was a minor miracle.

We were white as ghosts after the long northern winter, and all we wanted to do was lie in the hot Aussie sun and drink cold Aussie beer. I got burnt to a crisp, which made Bon laugh. We didn't talk to his parents about how we were doing or how bad things had been in London. Isa would never have pried and I didn't want to ruin our homecoming. It was all pushed aside. Isa asked her son what he planned to do back in Adelaide, but Bon didn't have much of an answer. Fraternity was in tatters, but they hadn't officially broken up. He assumed they'd start playing again when everyone had regrouped, or he'd find another band. There was no talk of changing careers or getting a day job. No one expected it.

There was probably a lot more going on under the surface than I could see, but Bon kept it all to himself. Part of my frustration with him was that whenever he was down, he was a closed shop - if something really serious was going on, you had to drag it out of him. I think he was entering a really lost period of his life, but I didn't have it in me to try and help him. I was just so relieved to be home.

We took the train from Perth to Adelaide, across the Nullarbor Plain. It was cheaper than flying. For two days, we looked at nothing but dust and desert, with the occasional rusty town sliding past the window. The landscape was as empty as London had been full, as dry as England had been cold and wet. It was a real shock to the system.

We spent most of the trip in the dining car, where Bon found a group of people and a guitar. They threw an impromptu train party to ring in the New Year. Bon played and sang and drank, and the whole car sang along with him. At night, the two of us curled up next to each other in the cabin. We were still affectionate with each other but the romance was gone. It was a jaded, beaten-up kind of love. There was no future in it.

My sisters were at the train station to meet us. Kathleen had a new baby with her, my nephew Steven, and he was quite a shy little kid. Bon went in with his usual gusto, pulling faces and squeezing the kid's cheeks.

'G'day! It's Uncle Bon! Graaaaaar,' he bellowed.

The poor kid hid his face in his Mum's hair and started bawling his eyes out.

'Sorry Bon,' Kathleen told him. 'He's not used to that sort of enthusiasm.'

We went back to Mum's place in Prospect; back to my old bedroom, with the two divans pushed together and Mum snoring softly across the hall. Fay had moved out while I was away.

I found secretarial work with a courier service in Mile End, Ward's Freight Services. Bon, without much else to do, went out and got himself a job at the Wallaroo Fertiliser Plant in Port Adelaide. He came home from his first day of work and told me he'd met a bloke called 'Bunny'.

'Bunny?' I said.

'His last name is Ouster,' Bon grinned.

It was our only whiff of a regular working-class routine. We got up in the morning, headed off to our jobs, clocked on and clocked off, and went home to Mum, who always had dinner on the table. Bon nearly broke his back, lugging shit around all day. I washed his work overalls, which were caked in fertiliser dust. They were horrible beige things that just never got clean. They spread a fine, gritty shit all over the house.

When Bon decided to get a new motorbike, Kathleen and her husband Barry went guarantor. They'd always liked Bon. The bike was a Suzuki 550 (not a Triumph, as they said later) and he bought it with finance from Custom Credit. It gave Bon a bit of freedom, at least.

Hamish threw a party at his place in North Adelaide to welcome Fraternity home. I didn't know what was happening with the band, but the party was a pretty bad omen. The night started out well - we had a great time sitting around the pool and catching up with a bunch of our old friends - but things took a tragic turn. Hamish's mother was on the second floor veranda, waving goodbye to the last of the guests, when she accidentally fell from the balcony and died. We didn't see it - no one really heard about it until the next day - but it left us all with a sick and sad feeling. Things weren't going right.

Bon had thrown everything he had into rock 'n' roll and it had let him down. He was crushed and deflated, like he had reached the end of the road.

We were at an outdoor concert back in Adelaide and a bloke Bon had known from the music industry walked straight past him without a second glance.

'Nobody wants to know about me anymore, 'Rene.'

He was twenty-seven. It seems so young now, but in the Seventies people that age were already stuck into their careers. They had houses and families. Bon didn't feel like he had anything to show for the last ten years, except a few tattoos. Not that he regretted anything. It's not like he pined for a normal life, he just thought he'd missed his chance with music. At twenty-seven he was like an old man in the music industry.

Bon's mood was darker when we got home, and he was drinking a lot more. At the fertiliser plant, he found another ready-made bunch of guys to party with and he partied all the time. The thing is, if you're a singer without a band, all that rock 'n' roll excess just looks like an alcohol problem. Bon just didn't want to grow up.

There was nothing going on with his music. The closest he came to a music career when we first got back was singing in a commercial for Axis Jeans. All he had to do was sing 'Axis Jeans for every girl and boy, joy, joy, joy!' He rehearsed it and rehearsed it, then rode off to the city for the recording. He got absolutely blind on the way home, pulled his bike up on the lawn, fell off the bike, and kept singing the jingle at the top of his lungs. 'Axis Jeans for every girl and boy, JOY, JOY, JOY!' It was funny, but it was also kind of sad.

We talked about getting a place of our own at one stage. Bon had been hanging out with a guy at work called Rick Lennon, and Bon suggested the three of us move in together - it never occurred to him that he and his wife should live alone. There were always people in between us, interfering - Bon had so many fans and friends and hangers-on - but it was that way because he wanted it that way. He just didn't want to settle down, that was never on the cards. I'm sure he loved me, but I'm equally sure he regretted getting married, at least at that point in his life. He was all over the place.

It was impossible to tell if he was having a good time, even when he was drinking. Bon's friends Bruce and Roz Barker threw a party one weekend and Bon, pissed out of his mind, climbed on to the roof of the shed and dived into the pool. He managed to split his lip, or cut his eye, and the first thing he did when he emerged from the water was rub blood all over his face and run into the crowd, growling and yelling like a maniac. It was meant to be funny. He was the centre of attention, as usual, but the whole thing was off. People cleared out of his path with a look of confusion on their faces. Bon hardly noticed, he was such a mess. At the end of the party, he got stuck into a water-bomb fight with a guy called Terry, just as we were trying to drag him into the car. We were all knackered and ready to leave but Bon was in his own world, laughing his head off. I felt like I was watching him through a window, like I wasn't really there.

He did his best to keep partying and push it all out of his head, but there were days when the booze made him feel worse rather than better. It was usually when I was having a go at him for drinking too much. We were over at Bruce and Anne's place for a barbecue, on yet another weekend, and Bon stood at their kitchen sink, getting darker and darker with every beer. He started making smart-arse comments and eventually they turned nasty. I was over it.

'I'm going,' I said.

'We'll go together on the bike.'

'I'm not getting on the bike with you, you're pissed,' I told him. 'I'll get a taxi.'

'You're not going in a fucking taxi.'

He followed me outside and we continued to argue. We were livid with each other. All the unspent rage from London was right under the surface, and it only took a little scratch to bring it up. I was still insisting I was getting a cab when Bon picked me up and started walking towards the motorbike. I shoved at his chest and screamed at him to let me go.

'Put me down, you bastard.'

'Yeah alright,' he said.

His arms fell without warning and dropped me like a ton of bricks on the concrete.

I was stunned. I stood up slowly and looked at him.

In that moment, I remembered a day before we left Adelaide, when Bon had been racing down Prospect Road in Hamish's old ute, hitting bumps from the filled-in spoon drains. *He's going fast*, I thought, *he's going really fast, he's got to turn right in a minute.* He flew into the corner and the passenger door swung open; I reached out to grab it, but it slipped out of my grasp. The door kept going and so did I, tumbling out of the car and bouncing off the footpath. Bon was horrified. He picked me up and carried me home, cooing like an old nurse.

'Are you alright, darling?' he'd said. 'Poor 'Rene, I'm so sorry.'

He'd been so gentle and motherly; it actually made me laugh.

The guy standing in front of me at Bruce and Anne's house had none of that tenderness left in his eyes. I turned my back and walked down the street to find a taxi, with tears rolling down my face.

Bon came home and apologised. I know he felt terrible for hurting me, but I think it made him face something he'd been trying to avoid. He was restless and unhappy. Things had been eating away at him, turning over in the back of his mind. It erupted in a way that made him ashamed of himself, but that eruption had cleared away all the rubble in his head. 'I don't want to do this anymore, Irene,' he said.

He told me he was moving in with Bruce and Anne, and within a few days he was gone.

I knew it was coming. I still loved him, but the romance was gone. I wanted things to be the way they had been in the beginning, but I didn't have any fight left in me. I didn't know how to make him happy. I felt like I had failed somehow, because I knew I would never meet another person like Bon. We were an even match. He wasn't weak but he wasn't arrogant. He was kind and affection-ate and funny; rough around the edges but with a good heart. And I knew he loved me. He just wasn't in love with me any-more.

Our relationship didn't have much of a chance. I like to think that if Fraternity had been successful in England, things would have been different with Bon and I, but maybe that's just wishful thinking. In all likelihood, it would have been something else down the track. One thing's for sure, he was never going to be OK until his career was OK. Music came first. Unfortunately, his career was in a worse state than our marriage. With Fraternity on indefinite hold, Bon started kicking around with Peter Beagley of Headband, a local blues-rock outfit that had had a decent run in the early Seventies. Headband broke up just as Bon returned from England, and Peter formed a new group called The Mount Lofty Rangers. He asked Bon to sing. They jammed together and wrote a few songs; a ballad about a prostitute ('Clarissa') and a tongue-in-cheek tune about wasted potential ('Been Up in the Hills Too Long'). Bon played roughly a dozen gigs with the group and recorded a couple of songs, one called 'Carey Gully' and one called 'Round and Round and Round'. The latter was released as a single decades later, along with video footage of Bon riding his motor-bike in the hills, but nothing much came of it at the time. The Rangers were one of those kick-around bands that musicians get into when they've got nothing else; they had more than one lead singer and dozens of guitarists and drummers passed through their ranks. Bon didn't take it seriously; he was just biding his time until the next opportunity came along.

I couldn't bear to stay at Mum's after he left. I didn't want to sit around licking my wounds. Fay was living with her boyfriend in Hackney but I knew she wasn't very happy. I asked her to get a place with me. I didn't tell Fay much about what had happened, I just told her Bon and I were separating and I needed to move out of Mum's. She was shocked; she really hadn't seen it coming. I'd done my best to hide my problems from Mum and Fay, to save my stupid pride.

'But you guys are great together,' Fay said. 'I don't understand.'

I could only shrug.

'It's over,' I said.

I think Fay was right, but it didn't matter anymore. Bon and I were too young. We didn't stand a chance.

Within a couple of weeks, Fay and I found a three-bedroom house in Stepney and I started a new life. I didn't see Bon for weeks. He cut the cord and that was it, radio silence. I didn't know what he was up to and I didn't want to ask about him, and our friends knew better than to get involved. They probably thought it was all for the best.

One afternoon, Vince and I drove around to see a friend of his called Rema. When we pulled up out the front of her house, we saw Bon's bike parked outside.

'Do you want to wait in the car?' Vince said.

I shook my head. I didn't want to see him, but I didn't want to hide in the car either. It seemed pathetic. Inside the house, we found Bon and Rema on the couch, watching television. I don't know if he was sleeping with her, but I wouldn't have been surprised. He barely looked up when I walked in.

'The spare helmet is at Mum's place,' I told him. 'I've moved out. You can pick it up whenever you like.'

'Yeah, alright. Thanks,' Bon said.

He wasn't rude, he was just distant. He chatted to Vince for a few minutes but his energy was flat. I don't know if it was because I was there. I felt so uncomfortable around him and he was obviously really uncomfortable being around me. It was a miserable scene.

The next time I was in the same room as Bon, he was in a coma. In six weeks, the only time I had spoken to him was that day at Rema's place. In hospital, he was silent. I stared at his broken body as the nurses moved around us, trying to recognise the man I knew in the mess of flesh lying still on the hospital bed. *But how could that be Bon?* His face was black and purple, and there were deep slashes on his throat. He had a broken arm, broken ribs and a smashed collarbone; half of his teeth were missing and his jaw was wired shut. He was completely mutilated.

I didn't understand what had happened, but at the same time I knew. He was drinking and he got on his bike. There was an accident.

Earlier that night - May 3, 1974 - Bon had had a band rehearsal with The Mount Lofty Rangers at a pub in North Adelaide. Vince Lovegrove was at the Old Lion Hotel when Bon turned up, pissed and belligerent. Vince said there was an argument and Bon had left, smashing a bottle of Jack Daniels on the ground before climbing on his motorbike and taking off at high speed.

It was past midnight when my doorbell rang. Fay and I had been out that evening and we'd arrived home less than half an hour earlier.

'Who the hell is that?' she said.

My heart slowed as I opened the door. Two policemen were standing on our front porch with that sombre, professional look they get when something is really wrong. I felt Fay move closer to me.

'We're looking for the nearest relative of Ronald Belford Scott,' one of the officers said.

'I'm his wife,' I replied.

'Mrs Scott, your husband has been in a motorcycle accident. He's at the Queen Elizabeth but I'm afraid it's very serious. You'll need to go to the hospital.'

The blood drained out of my face. I started shaking, and then I was sobbing. Fay hurried over to put her arms around me.

'Something's happened to Bon,' I told her.

There was no phone and we didn't have a car. Fay ran to the phone booth and called a taxi, but we waited for ages and it never came. In the end we had to flag down a passing car and hitchhike into town. I had pulled myself together, but my stomach was full of knots. I thought I might be sick. I had no idea what state Bon would be in by the time we got there - I didn't even know if he would last that long.

The hospital was in complete chaos. Bon was in emergency but they wouldn't let us through. We had to strain to catch a glimpse of him through the swinging double doors.

He thrashed on the bed while nurses rushed around with packs of blood and doctors barked instructions. I saw his face but he was barely recognisable, a bloodied pool of smashed jelly. It was absolutely horrifying. He was moaning in pain.

'That's my husband!' I told them, but a nurse pushed me aside.

'We're taking him to theatre,' she said.

We waited. It seemed like hours that Bon was in there, but the nurses came out periodically with reports. *He's stopped bleeding; he's stabilised.* In the meantime, we phoned the people we could. I called Isa and Vince; Fay called Mum and Kathleen. In the early hours of the morning, they moved Bon to the intensive care unit and we were finally allowed to see him.

We found him pale and limp under the strip lighting. There were severe internal injuries on top of all the broken bones, so the doctors had put him in an induced coma. They didn't think he could deal with the pain. He looked so small and ruined on that bed, I didn't blame them. It wasn't Bon. Bon was fit, wiry and strong. The person on the bed looked like a little child.

When Kathleen and Mum turned up at the hospital, they were both close to tears. Kathleen gave a little speech by Bon's bedside.

'He's a lovely little fella, he doesn't deserve this,' she announced. 'We should all join hands and say a prayer for him.'

Fay stood up next to me and said 'Cigarette?'

Vince had already arrived and we left him standing awkwardly as my mother and sister began communing with God. We stopped at the reception desk to collect Bon's things and the nurse handed us his helmet, smashed along the jaw line and covered in blood.

'I'm so sorry,' she said.

It was clear she thought that Bon had died.

'He's still here!' Fay answered, rolling her eyes.

For the next few days, I sat beside Bon's bed and waited for him to come around, holding his hand or reaching out to brush his arm. He was struggling to breathe. There were tubes and wires criss-crossing his body, which was covered in bandages. I felt terrified and helpless, and the doctors didn't say much to reassure me. As long as Bon was in the coma, it was touch and go.

My sisters took time off work and came to the hospital. Kathleen was with me one day when Bon's heart monitor stopped.

'Oh Christ,' she said, and started screaming for help.

The nurse on duty rushed in and started thumping him in the chest.

'Come on, Ron, come on,' she said.

I thought a rib would crack, but she kept at it until the line on the monitor sprung to life again.

I came in the next morning and the nurse on duty told me Bon was coming round.

'We've had the odd word out of him,' she laughed. 'He says he's a singer.'

By the end of the day Bon was fully conscious, although he probably wished he wasn't. He was in a lot of pain.

'When are we going home?' he asked me. I told him I had moved in with Fay. 'Is there enough room for my bike?' he said.

I laughed and told him we'd figure it out.

Bon was in the hospital for almost three weeks. Initially I stayed with him around the clock, and when he was stronger I went back to work and visited him in the evenings. He was loaded with painkillers and out of it most of the time. When he was less groggy, I asked him what had happened the night of the accident. All he remembered was flying over the handlebars; he said he didn't see what hit him. Bon didn't tell me he was drunk, but Vince had told me the whole story by then.

If Bon felt sorry for himself, you couldn't see it in his face. You couldn't see his face at all; it was covered in metal scaffolding. He was drinking his food through a straw. He lost a heap of weight, very quickly, and became terribly frail.

When he was well enough to get out of bed, he shuffled around the room in a dark blue hospital dressing gown, hunched over like an old man. They didn't set his shoulder properly; it was just a little bit curved for the rest of his life.

'He's a very sick boy,' the doctor told me. 'He's going to need a lot of care.'

There was no discussion about where Bon would go when he got out of hospital. Fay and I collected him on the day he was released, bundled him into a cab and took him back to the house at Stepney. They had sent him home in a hospital dressing gown, barefoot. His jaw was still wired shut and they hadn't given us wire-cutters. I was terrified Bon would vomit and then choke to death.

Bon started complaining about stomach pains a couple of days after we got him home and began to cough up blood. I rushed him back to the hospital in a taxi. I was yelling for help when we got to emergency but it was jammed with people and the nurses all had their hands full. I had to grab the nearest thing I could find, a kidney-shaped metal tray, and hold it under Bon's mouth as he spewed red fluid and mucus. It had subsided by the time the doctors saw him so they sent him home again the same day.

Isa flew over from Perth when Bon came out of hospital and moved into our spare bedroom for a couple of weeks. She stayed home with Bon while I was at work and cooked for us every day, and when it got cold she bought us a heater. Bon started wearing my Dad's old air force jacket around the house; a hand-made sheepskin coat with a huge tear on the arm. He looked pathetic in it, but it kept him warm.

Having Isa around was a real gift - it stopped me feeling anxious when I went off to work in the morning. Isa knew that Bon and I had separated but she didn't breathe a word about it because she knew he needed my help. She would never suggest taking him back to Perth because he'd never agree to go. It was enough for her to be there briefly, when he came home, to help him back on his feet again.

Slowly, Bon started to mend. Weeks passed and the bruises faded. He couldn't move very well, but he could stand and walk, and take care of himself well enough while I was out of the house. The light crept back into his face.

I was sharing a bed with him again, but it wasn't the same. He was my responsibility, not my lover. If it had been years down the track it would have been different, but Bon and I were still married. I looked after him without complaining because I cared about him very deeply, but it wasn't some hospital-bed romance. I couldn't let myself love him anymore. In the weeks that we had been apart, I had grown another layer of skin. I had forced myself to stop caring. It was strange having him back in my bed - it didn't feel completely natural anymore.

As time went on and Bon began to look like his old self, I started going out. I'd made a few friends around Stepney and we began hanging out at a bar called The Tivoli. Bon obviously wasn't happy about it. He'd ask me where I was headed and he'd wait up to see what time I got back. I caught him peeking through the curtains one night to see who had driven me home. On another night, he followed me to the pub and caught me chatting with a really great-looking guy I knew (coincidentally, also the most boring guy I'd ever met). Bon was ropeable.

I can't explain his jealousy. I guess when people are vulnerable and they feel knocked around, they reach out for what they know. Bon's life had totally collapsed at that point; his band was gone, his bike was gone and his body was completely fucked. I guess he thought I was the only thing he had left, and it made him a little crazy. I didn't take it too seriously. Something told me his attention wouldn't last.

When Graeme heard about the accident, he made plans to come and see his brother. He left his ship in Melbourne and drove across to Adelaide, and moved into the third bedroom of our house. There were four of us then - Bon and I, Fay and Graeme - and sometime in the middle of all of this, Fay and Graeme hit it off. It didn't take long. Graeme was very handsome and Fay was very attractive, so it was probably inevitable. Bon thought it was hilarious.

'Welcome to the family,' he laughed. 'And good fuckin' luck.'

Graeme wasn't a deep, dark, reflective sort of guy; he was

very easy-going and tended to accept things as they came. It was great having him around. Things fell into a bit of a happy routine with the four of us in the house. I sat the public service entrance exam and moved from the freight company back to the Civil Aviation Authority. Bon started to get out every now and again, though he was still pretty weak. Bruce, Uncle and John Freeman were jamming and Bon sat in on a few of their rehearsals. The News wrote a story about Fraternity getting back together, and the guys made some noise about recording a new album. Nothing came of it, of course.

In July, we threw a party for Bon's 28th birthday - a big celebration, because he was finally back on his feet. Bon wore a ball-hugging pair of overalls that Fay had taken in for him.

'Can you make them a bit tighter?' he'd asked.

'Where?' she'd replied.

'Everywhere.'

On the day of the party, I organised a ton of booze and stood at the kitchen bench making food while Bon was at the table rolling spliffs.

'She does the cooking and I carve the joints,' he joked.

He was handing out weed to everyone who walked through the door.

Bon smoked like a diesel engine while he recuperated, out of boredom more than anything else. It felt like he was going through five bags of weed a week, although he weathered it pretty well. I stayed away from dope because it made me too paranoid and Fay wasn't a big fan. It was a bit of a guy's hobby around our house.

A friend of Fay's came to pick her up for basketball practice one night and Bon offered the girl some hash.

'No thanks,' she told him. 'I've already eaten.'

Bon nearly busted a rib laughing. He was getting his old sense of humour back. I'll never forget the day he presented me with a new house plant; a metre-high cactus that stood stiff as a prick in its little pot.

'I bought this for ya,' he grinned. 'If you don't like it, you know where you can stick it.'

115

(I gave the cactus to Mum, who kept it on the front porch long enough for grow up to the roof snake along underneath, like some creepy bloody triffid.)

When he wasn't smoking weed, and sometimes when he was, Bon made pancakes. As the winter kicked in, he would disappear up to the hills with his mates to hunt for magic mushrooms, then he'd come home and make pancakes for everyone - breakfast, lunch or dinner. Hash cakes were another favourite. Bon fed one to my sister as she rushed off to work one day and Fay barely made it through the shift. She had a job washing dishes and making terrible seafood cocktails, but she kept dropping the plates. When she finally got home, Fay was ready to go out and party but she found Bon and Graeme asleep on the couch, victims of the hash cakes.

As his body healed, Bon's vanity was also on the mend. He was always a bit of a preener and he was completely unapologetic about it, like the day he finished a bottle of my 'no more tangle' hair spray.

'Did you seriously go through this whole bottle?!' I asked him.

Bon shrugged. 'You don't want me to have tangles, do ya?'

On a different morning, Bon was late for a dentist appointment and I was virtually pushing him out of the house.

'You've gotta go, you're gonna be late.'

Bon raced out the door and jumped into a waiting car and pulled away, and a second later I heard him screeching back up the drive. *Bang* went the car door, in raced Bon.

'Quick, where's your make-up?' he said.

'What?!'

"I can't see the dentist with this pimple on my face,' he said. 'It'll scare the shit out of him.'

The more Bon's mood improved, the nicer it was to have him around. He and I would curl up on the couch together and fall asleep, and all the bullshit and bitterness just melted away. We were in this suspended animation, not moving forward but with no expectations, and we learnt to like each other again. I knew deep down the marriage was stuffed; I just didn't worry about it much anymore. I figured whatever happened would happen.

The only thing we argued about was money. Bon's bike was written off in the accident, but he still had to make payments on it and I was on his case about it all the time because Kathleen and Barry were responsible if Bon defaulted on the loan. (Months later he called to tell me he was making his last payment to Custom Credit. 'I'd like to deliver it through their window,' he said, 'Wrapped around a brick.')

I bought a $90 FB Holden from a work colleague so that Bon could get around. With transport, he could get stuck into things again. Vince was running a booking agency called Jovan and Bon started to work for him, odd jobs here and there. Bon painted the Jovan office, then started bill-posting for the gigs, and every now and then Vince had him driving bands around. Vince was booking most of the major acts that came through Adelaide - Lobby Loyde and the Coloured Balls, Skyhooks and Buster Brown, with the odd international act thrown in - and I think it made Bon happy to be part of the music business in some way. But it was a far cry from what he really wanted to be doing. He wanted to be in the band, not driving them around.

As he got his strength back, Bon started singing again. It was a miracle that he could sing at all with all the scars on his neck, but his voice was as powerful as ever. It was just different. He had a particular kind of tone when he sang with Fraternity, a warmth around the high notes, but it was gone after the accident. Bon could scream and snarl with the best of them, but I missed his old voice. It was never the same.

He was determined to get back into music, he just needed the right opportunity. I could sense that he was restless, but there was nothing I could do to help him. It wasn't us - we were fine. Bon and I weren't in love but we weren't tearing each other to pieces. We were good friends who shared a bed and looked out for each other. It just wasn't what he needed.

The first time Bon saw AC/DC was in August 1974. They came through Adelaide with the Lou Reed and Stevie Wright tour and played their own show at the Pooraka Hotel. Bon was in stitches; he loved the little guitarist with his school uniform and backpack, but he thought they were a gimmick act. Most people did.

AC/DC played catchy rhythm and blues songs, but they weren't a gimmick. They were an up-and-coming group out of Sydney with a serious pedigree. The backbone of the band was a pair of amazing guitar players, Malcolm and Angus Young - the younger brothers of George Young from The Easybeats, who was at one point one of the biggest pop stars in Australia. The Easybeats had had a massive international hit in 1966 with 'Friday on My Mind' and George had gone on to become one of the most prolific and successful songwriters in the country. He wrote songs for half the music acts around in the Sixties and Seventies, including The Valentines. In 1974, he had another massive hit with 'Evie', sung by the former Easybeats frontman Stevie Wright. George Young was one of the greatest musical talents in the country.

Malcolm and Angus Young were probably just as talented as their older brother, but they were green by comparison. They had played guitar since they were kids, but their band had barely been together a year when Bon first saw them - although they'd manage to knock out a decent single in that time. 'Can I Sit Next to You Girl' was a glam-rock tune with muscly guitar work. Bon didn't mind the song, but he hated the singer. So did the Youngs, unfortunately. By the time AC/DC came through Adelaide in August, George Young had put the word out that the band wanted to replace their lead singer, a guy called Dave Evans. George and Vince knew each other well, and Vince suggested Bon. George remembered Bon from The Valentines and Fraternity. He could see the potential.

The first time I saw AC/DC was at the Pooraka Hotel in September. They were amazing, even back then. It was like nothing I'd ever heard, and Angus and Malcolm were just incredible to watch. It's like they were locked into each other. They were playing to the typical pissed Pooraka audience, but the crowd went crazy because the energy on stage was just electric. Angus threw himself around like a little maniac, dressed in his old school uniform. I was standing off to one side of the stage, but the room was so packed I was getting shoved all over the place.

'Get up there, Bon,' Vince kept saying.

The band didn't have a singer that night, and they were playing instrumental versions of old rock 'n' roll standards. The boys ripped through all these classic numbers and then finally, with enough pressure from Vince, Bon climbed on to the stage. I didn't think anything of it - it had been a while, but Bon used to do that sort of thing all the time, get up and sing a couple of tunes with the band. I didn't realise that AC/DC had just sacked Dave Evans and they wanted Bon to replace him.

I don't remember what he sang, but it was nothing like Fraternity. Fraternity seemed very old compared to AC/DC. They took themselves really seriously and they wrote serious music. It was great, but it could drone sometimes. AC/DC played this loud, unapologetic rock that nearly blew your head off, and Bon's voice just clicked right into it. He was just as loud as the band, hollering some old blues-rock standard - maybe 'Johnny B. Goode'? - at the top of his lungs. He sang his guts out.

At the end of the gig, Bon introduced me to the Youngs. The whole band was standing around at the side of the stage, laughing and slapping each other on the back, obviously very pleased with themselves. Everyone was on a high, Bon included. Malcolm and Angus were young and small but they had a lovely way about them; they were really friendly towards me, and Bon had obviously taken a shine to them. Like Bon, the Youngs were Scottish, so there was an instant bond. And there was some kind of magic connection with the band. I think Bon knew he was on to a winner.

I had no idea where all of this was heading. I didn't know that Bon had seen AC/DC play at the Pooraka a month earlier. I didn't know that he'd gone backstage to meet the band. I didn't know that Angus and Malcolm had called him an old man and challenged him to rock their balls off (or whatever the hell was said at the time); I didn't know that Bon had auditioned for them at Bruce Howe's place; I didn't know that AC/DC would sack Dave Evans a couple of weeks later. I didn't know all these cogs were turning that would take Bon out of my life. And I certainly had no bloody idea that history was being made. Bon looked genuinely, deeply happy, for the first time in a long time. And I was happy for him.

A few days later, he called me at work to tell me he was joining the band.

'How do you feel about moving to Sydney?' he asked.

I had a sinking feeling. I didn't stop to examine it, I just told Bon I would go, that I could apply for a transfer with work. But my heart wasn't in it. The thought of following Bon on another rock 'n' roll adventure made me tired. I don't know why I said yes. I don't know why he even asked, really - we'd just fallen into the habit of being together again. Bon assumed I would follow him because I was his wife, and I agreed because I thought I should. But I felt numb. He hadn't been that excited for a very long time. I didn't want to bring him down.

Bon left Adelaide at the end of September to join AC/DC in Sydney. I was going to follow him over as soon as he found a place and my transfer came through, but in the meantime AC/DC would be back in Adelaide in October. He was just going to suss things out; he'd be home in a few weeks.

Bon packed a bag, kissed me goodbye and said, 'See you soon, 'Rene.'

That was it. There was no pensive staring off of a pier while he weighed up his options; no cutting ties with his old life and riding off into the sunset. Nothing that dramatic. There was no suggestion at all that Bon and I were about to break up, except for the fact that we already had.

When Bon got to Sydney he stayed with AC/DC's manager, a guy called Dennis Laughlin. He met the Young clan and started jamming with the guys, knocking together some of the first real AC/DC tunes. In early October, he had his proper debut. His first real gig with AC/DC was at the Rockdale Masonic Hall on the south side of Sydney and they blew everyone away - according to Bon, anyway. He called me the next day, thrilled with himself.

'They fuckin' love me,' he crowed.

Angus said Bon's voice was like a hurricane that night, like the old man had something to prove.

After their Sydney shows, the band went back on tour. The first stop was Melbourne, where AC/DC was booked to play the Hard Rock Café gay night on October 16. Michael Browning was the promoter there; a couple of weeks later he would take over from Dennis Laughlin as AC/DC's manager. Meanwhile, the guys were headed back to Adelaide to play three nights at the Largs Pier Hotel.

I was at work when Bon drove into Adelaide. He was going to stop in at the house, drop off his things, then head off to the Largs Pier in the afternoon, and I was supposed to meet him there after work. When I got home that evening, Bon's bag was in the hallway and the rent money had disappeared from the kitchen drawer. I absolutely lost it.

It's not like Bon had been living out of my pocket, and it wasn't really like him to make off with a big pile of money like that, but it wasn't his money. The fact that it was our rent money was a very big deal to me. Fay and I were very responsible with paying our rent on time. It was something we took seriously. Of course Bon wouldn't understand something like that because he hadn't paid rent in years. He just sponged off me or whoever else was around.

I don't know if it was fair or reasonable, but something inside of me snapped. Suddenly I was back in London again, scrimping and saving to make ends meet while Bon was off dicking around with a band. And the first thing he does when he gets home is take our rent money? *I don't fucking think so.* All the old, rancid anger came flooding back; all that stuff about London that I'd never really dealt with because Bon had never really apologised. I was furious. It was probably an overreaction, to be honest. Bon was my husband, and in all likelihood he had just grabbed the cash in a hurry as he was running out the door. But I was going to let him have it anyway.

I jumped in a cab and sped off down to the Pier and stormed right up to the stage. AC/DC were in the middle of their first set. It was the first time that I saw them play their own material, but don't ask me how they sounded. I wasn't standing there with my arms folded, tapping my foot and admiring Bon's moves. I was fuming. My dear husband was facing a room full of pissed admirers and one very crazy-looking woman with glowering eyes and steam coming out of her ears.

I made a beeline for Bon during the break and the poor bastard actually looked happy to see me for a second. The smile died on his face just as I started yelling.

'How could you take the bloody rent money? What the fuck is wrong with you?'

Bon looked confused for a second and then belligerent. He wasn't the sort of person to back down.

'I didn't have any money,' he said.

He didn't apologise or offer anything like a reasonable explanation, which drove me mad. I started screaming even louder and he started yelling back, and the two of us made a very ugly scene right outside the stage door. I doubt anyone heard us over the roar of the pub, but it was pretty spectacular, though it didn't last long. I said what I had to say and I left, and that was the end of it. I was done arguing with him.

Bon didn't come home that night and I didn't care - the sooner he was out of my life the better. When I got back from the Largs, I asked Fay to help me pack his stuff.

'Don't give him the good suitcase!' she said. 'Give him the shit suitcase!'

When he turned up the next day, he found me in the back yard, lying in the sun. Bon threw a wad of cash in my direction. *I was always going to give it back.*

'That's it,' he said. 'It's over.'

I shrugged and said, 'Your bag's already packed.'

I know it's petty, but I've always been glad that I had the last word.

PART THREE

BON SCOTT'S EX

⚡

CHAPTER 7

I wasn't sad when Bon left that day. It was a relief to know our relationship was finally, truly over. The whole thing had dragged on for so long past its use-by date that we were just spent. There were no desperate phone calls or apologies; we both just knew it was done.

When they left Adelaide, AC/DC went back to Sydney via Melbourne. They did a management deal with Michael Browning, who absorbed all of the band's debts and started paying them a weekly wage. In Sydney, Bon signed his publishing rights over to AC/DC's record label and the band went into the studio. With George Young and his partner Harry Vanda behind the desk, AC/DC made their debut album. They had been together about six weeks; High Voltage was recorded in 10 days.

I don't remember how long it took for Bon to start calling me at work, but it wasn't more than a few weeks. After a few weeks, he unilaterally decided that we were going to be mates, and we were, and that was it. I had a few cracks at him over his motorcycle debt to Custom Credit, but I was glad to hear his voice. After all the bullshit and the bitterness were done, he was still my closest friend. Bon felt the same way. Things were going great with the band and he wanted to tell me all about it.

'Wait 'til you hear the record, 'Rene, it's a fucking ripper,' he laughed.

I didn't miss Bon. I had really felt it in the weeks between him walking out and having the bike accident, but I was OK when he left for good. I just wasn't sure what to do next. I put a hold on my transfer at work but I didn't cancel it. I felt like I needed a change but I wasn't really sure what kind, so I did nothing and life went on regardless. I hung out with Vince a lot, and his new wife Helen. Helen was really sharp, with a lovely dry wit, and I thought really highly of her. Vince was great. He kept a really close eye on me and made sure I wasn't wallowing in self-pity.

'Come out tonight 'Reenie, I've got a band on at the Pier... come over 'Rene, we're having a party with this band down from Sydney.'

Bon was gone but I had our old friends around me, and a few new ones as well. Vince had started managing a band called Cold Chisel and they quickly became regulars on the scene. They were lovely guys. The singer was a kid called Jim Barnes, who was so awkward he had to turn his back on the audience whenever he performed. The drummer was an English guy called Steve Prestwich, and the guitarist was a shy young man called Ian Moss. There was a pianist too, a bloke named Don Walker, but he was away at uni when I met the rest of the band.

Cold Chisel hadn't been together much more than a year. They were all very young but they were incredibly talented; Jim and Ian had these amazing voices that complimented each other beautifully. Vince was really excited about them, although Don was a bit of an unknown factor. The guys talked about Don like he was the second coming. He was the intellectual and the songwriter; the rest of the band really looked up to him.

Ian was nineteen when I met him. Vince obviously thought that the fastest way for me to get over Bon was to get with someone else, because he was hell-bent on getting Ian and I together. We were watching the guys play at the Largs Pier one night when I turned to Vince and said, 'Ian's very cute, isn't he?'

The next thing I knew, Vince was over in Ian's ear. "Reenie really likes you, Ian. She does. She does, she does, she does, she does.'

So that sorted that out really quickly. I felt like an old lady compared to Ian, but it was a breath of fresh air to be with someone with a really light load on their shoulders. He was sweet and smart and easy-going, and there was absolutely no pressure. I knew there was no future in it because Ian was just *so young*, or at least he seemed that way to me. He was nineteen and I was an old lady at twenty-three, but we had a lot of fun together. Ian had a really nutty sense of humour. He picked up Fay's cat one day and popped it on top of the ironing board, then gave it a gentle press with the (cold) iron.

'Now don't get creased again,' he muttered.

We would lie around for hours talking nonsense to each other, giggling to ourselves over the most random and terrible jokes.

'You little chicken,' he would say to me. 'You redundant little cabbage patch.'

Sometimes we'd entertain ourselves by clucking at each other like chickens - embarrassing but true.

Being with Ian was very, very different to the way I'd felt with Bon. Bon shook my cage; he was like a sparring partner. I had a deep love with Bon that also happened to be deeply annoying. Ian was a lovely combination of wit and silliness, all right there on the surface. We seemed to spend most of our time in bed. When Don came back from school and moved in with Ian, into a new place in the suburb of Cowandilla, he graciously put up with me as his unofficial extra housemate. Don watched the whole affair with a sardonic eye.

'Ian's up,' I told him one day, knowing the two of them had somewhere to be.

'Naturally he would be up,' Don remarked dryly, 'At this time of the morning.'

Like Ian, Don had a great sense of the ridiculous.

AC/DC made their first appearance on Countdown on November 29, 1974. Countdown had only just started, but there was really nothing else like it in Australia, a weekly music show where you could see all the latest Australian bands playing all the latest Australian music. On the fourth episode, AC/DC played 'Baby, Please Don't Go', an old blues classic covered by Muddy Waters and Them, which they would later release as a single. Bon wore a shark's tooth in his ear, which I had bought for him at the Portobello markets in London. He liked it because he'd seen Keith Richards wearing something similar.

A couple of weeks after Bon's Countdown debut, I turned 24. I spent my birthday at the pub, happily pissed with my new boyfriend and the rest of our Adelaide friends. Ian gave me a present; a little toy mouse holding a piece of cheese that he hung from the lighting fixture in my hallway. He snuck into my house to install it and polished off a bottle of wine while he was there, and left the empty bottle on the hallway table with a calling card scribbled on the label.

126

'Buck buck buck,' it read. 'Buck buck buck buck.'

Fay and I had decided to move to the other side of town. I wanted a change of scenery, but I was worried that no one would come and visit us down at Henley Beach.

'I'll visit you,' Ian told me.

As we planned our move across town, AC/DC relocated from Sydney to Melbourne. Along with Malcolm and teenager Angus, who had never lived out of home before, Bon moved into a place on Lansdowne Road in Prahran. By all accounts, the boys went completely feral and slept with everything in sight.

AC/DC were playing gigs all over town, for whatever audiences would have them. They played to teenyboppers one night and the gay crowd the next, and everywhere they went they made new fans. Many of the fans were female and many of them ended up back at Lansdowne Road, or so the story goes. Bon didn't share those gory details with me. He talked about the band, and how well everything was going. He was still in a bit of pain from the accident, he said, but he felt about ten years younger. He said he was partying a lot.

Back in Adelaide, Fay and Graeme were still going strong. Graeme treated Fay very well, bringing her presents and flying her over to meet his ship whenever he was in port. In December, they spent a weekend in Melbourne together and Graeme took Fay to visit his brother in Lansdowne Road. Fay came back with a full report but it wasn't very interesting. She said Angus and Bon sat very politely in the living room playing his guitar and Bon offered her a cup of tea - if there were groupies about, they must have been hiding under the bed.

Bon's friend Mary Walton had invited him around for a meal and he brought Fay and Graeme along with him. The three of them turned up on Mary's doorstep at five o'clock in the evening.

'We're here for dinner,' Bon said.

'It was supposed to be lunch,' she laughed. 'You're three hours late.'

Mary was an old friend of Bon's from his days in The Valentines and he'd been seeing her quite a bit since he moved back to Melbourne. He was always a sucker for a home-cooked meal.

Later that night, Fay and Graeme saw AC/DC play at the

Southside Six Hotel. She came home with tales of Angus clambering over tables and scaling the bar like a tiny mountain goat. They were both really impressed, particularly Graeme.

By Christmas, AC/DC were back on the road, touring the countryside in an old Ansett Clipper bus. Bon spent Christmas in a motel room in rural South Australia; I spent Christmas with Vince and Helen. They had a bunch of people over for the day, including Fay and I, and all the guys from Cold Chisel. After a few drinks, the boys started singing Christmas carols with these lovely vocal harmonies. It was lovely. Ian and I spent the rest of the day curled up on the floor, like a pair of teenagers.

In early January, Fay and I moved into our new place, which was a couple of streets back from Henley Beach. We had a lovely lady next door who liked to stick her nose over the fence and chat, until the day she saw Graeme's dope plant in the back garden.

'What's that?' she said. 'I haven't seen that before.'

I had always wanted to live near the beach and it made for a nice change after everything that had happened. Plenty of people came to visit, probably too many in fact. The guys from Chisel often landed at our place after a show to drink the night away. I woke up to find a note in my letterbox one day: *The residents of this street also enjoy music, but they are sick to death of hearing yours at 3 o'clock in the morning.*

The Largs Pier was just up the road and Fay and I spent even more time there after we moved, if that was even possible. We were over at the Largs when Bon appeared on our doorstep, pissed and hollering at the locked front door.

'I've fucking come here to see you and you're not fucking here!' he shouted.

The next-door neighbour told us all about it - she was absolutely terrified.

The following night we went back to the Largs to see AC/DC play. (Graeme took a photo of me getting ready to go, standing in my tights in front of the bathroom mirror with half my lipstick on and a very annoyed expression on my face.) The band was even tighter than I remembered and they put on a fantastic show. Angus was climbing all over the stage and Bon was just a bundle of energy, stomping all over the place. He was a totally different performer. When he was in Fraternity, you'd always see Bon putting a finger to his ear to check that he was hitting the notes. There wasn't a lot of that going on with AC/DC. There was a lot of thrusting and grinning from Bon, and dirty looks for the girls in the front row. It really made me laugh.

At the end of the gig, Bon handed me a record; a 12-inch test pressing in a plain white wrapper.

'It's our album,' he said. 'It's brilliant.'

'Of course it is,' I grinned.

High Voltage had eight tracks, including AC/DC's cover of 'Baby, Please Don't Go'. One of the tracks ('Soul Stripper') had been written by Malcolm and Angus before Bon joined the band; the other six they wrote together. It was early days for AC/DC but they already had a distinctive sound and the guitars on High Voltage were great. It didn't pack the same punch as the band's live show, but it was still a lot heavier than most of the stuff that was coming out. *It's about time*, I thought. The world didn't need one more folk singer.

My test pressing of High Voltage included a track that didn't make it on to the final version of the album called 'Love Song'. It was like a throwback to something Bon would have written in The Valentines, so I'm not surprised they left it out, although personally I thought it was quite lovely. It was a ballad to a girl named Jean.

'I picked Jean because it's a good Scottish name,' Bon told me.

He seemed a bit embarrassed about the track, like he was looking for my approval. I got the feeling that if I'd said I liked it, Bon would too, and if I said it was shit, he'd agree. Everywhere else on the album, his voice was very dirty. I missed the tone he used to have with Fraternity, but the snarl he developed for AC/DC really suited the lyrics. He'd dug through his notebooks and come up with some excellent toilet poetry on his two favourite subjects, rock 'n' roll and sex. Overall I thought he'd done a decent job; there were only a couple of tunes on the album that I really didn't like. 'Little Lover' was sleazy and slow and 'She's Got Balls' was worse; there was something about that song that just rubbed me the wrong way. Not that it was anything personal. I had no idea, not for a very long time, that Bon told people that song was about me.

Years later, I read an AC/DC fan's version of events and it went something like this: *Irene asked Bon to write a song about her. He wrote 'She's Got Balls', so she left him.*

Is that right?! I thought to myself. *Well at least she had a good reason.*

By late January, AC/DC were back in Melbourne and recruiting a new drummer, Phil Rudd (ex-Buster Brown). At the end of the month, they picked up a gig at the 1975 Sunbury Festival, which would have been their biggest crowd yet. Thirty-thousand beer-swilling music fans descended on a farm in country Victoria to see a huge line-up of rock bands, including Sherbet, Daddy Cool and Billy Thorpe & The Aztecs. Skyhooks played but they were still fairly new and the crowd didn't know what to make of them. Queen came over from England and suffered even worse; they got booed off of the stage. The headline act was Deep Purple, but there was some controversy around how much they were paid for the gig. AC/DC were pulled in at the last minute, when it looked like Deep Purple might pull out. In the end, the headline act went on as scheduled and AC/DC were supposed to follow, but the minute their set finished the Deep Purple crew started dismantling the stage. Michael Browning told the band to get out there anyway and the whole thing turned into a massive brawl.

Bon told me all about it the next time he called, although I'd already read about it in the newspapers. He loved Deep Purple. Bon was blown away when we saw them play in Adelaide, so he really took it hard. He was torn between disbelief and disgust, not just because he admired the band so much but because somehow AC/DC were blamed for everything going wrong.

High Voltage was released officially in mid-February. The cover gave me a decent laugh; it was a cartoon of a dog having a piss against a high-voltage power station. In March, the guys put out 'Love Song' as a single, with 'Baby, Please Don't Go' as the B-side. I don't remember ever hearing 'Love Song' on the radio, but the B-side was everywhere in a matter of weeks. I couldn't get away from it. AC/DC played it live on Countdown at the end of March and then again in April, and every time I saw them on the telly, Bon looked slightly more ridiculous. He had cut his hair for the first appearance, which looked pretty terrible.

In April, he was dressed as a schoolgirl. He had this awful blonde wig, fake boobs and a ton of make-up, and a black bangle hooped through his sleeper earring. *There he goes again*, I thought. I really had no idea what he was thinking. He had morphed from this very sexy rock 'n' roll singer into a painted clown, just for the shock value, and all I could do was roll my eyes. But I wasn't much of a judge of popular opinion. People went crazy for it - 'Baby, Please Don't Go' was in the chart for 25 weeks.

Off stage, Bon was running wild. He started dating a seventeen-year-old girl called Judy King, who was using heroin. He didn't mention her drug habit to me, just her haircut.

'You should cut your hair,' he told me during one of his calls.

'This chick I'm seeing has really short hair and it looks fantastic.'

Bon didn't tell me he had a brawl with Judy's dad on the front lawn of the Lansdowne Road place. I had to read about that in the newspaper. 'Popstar, Brunette and a Bed: Then Her Dad Turned Up!' screamed the headline. My eyes nearly fell out of my head. I gave Bon plenty of shit about it the next time he called. I told him that if he didn't want to get beaten up by angry fathers he should stop chasing teenage girls.

'I don't chase them,' he laughed. 'They chase me.'

The other thing Bon neglected to mention was that he'd almost died of an overdose. A couple of weeks earlier, Judy had given him a cap of morphine. His band-mate found him face down and blue on the floor of his bedroom, with Judy and her girl-friend nearly hysterical beside him. I don't know why he didn't tell me. He might have been embarrassed, or he might not have wanted me to worry. I didn't find out about it until years later, when I became friends with Judy and her sister Betty. They were both junkies, but they were nice girls. Judy was absolutely beautiful and she'd been a star athlete when she was younger. It broke their Mum's heart to see them throw their lives away.

'Why don't you get on the booze like Irene and give up the bloody drugs,' she would tell them.

But it was easier said than done.

May 3, 1975
Irene Scott
4 Franklin St Henley Beach South Australia

From:
Room 410, Squire Inn Bondi Junction NSW
(Be here for another week Graeme)

G'day spunk & sister & brother,

How are you all. It's Friday up here in Sydney. Were playin up here for 3 weeks, which is something I've been lookin forward to for a while. Melbourne ain't no place for any cunt with a bit of sence & I think we qualify. Times is tough at the moment cause Carouso 'ere 'as lost 'is vocal sound. Know wat I meen. Worked so hard this last few weeks its just said fuck you lot I'm havin a rest. Had to cancel a weeks work but because we're in Sydney we can spend all out time in Alberts recording our next smash (with a bullet).

Have you <u>bought</u> a copy of the record yet or did Faye get the one from the record shop. That was only a test pressin & won't last a month anyway so you'll have to buy one. I can't even get one for myself or you'd have it. I just bought a "new" ZZ Top LP (Rio Grande Mud) & it's a beaut. The other one (Tres Hombre) (have you got it yet) is a little bit better?

I miss ya sometimes 'Rene. Strange that comin from me but it's true (but only sometimes). It's probably the weather.

Buy a copy of the next (or the next next) Ram. It's like the new hippy come music come underground come cum paper in Aust. But they interviewed us the other day and we might have said something interestin.

Don't know if you're already into him but B.C is !!! It's the cartoon story ya know but this guys great, better than most. I borrowed a whole stack from Angus' brother & I love them. They're written by a bloke called Johnny Hart. Good stuff.

Ok that's all your gonna get this time. Give my love to Cathlene & regards to Barry. Hope all's well for them. Thanks for the fifty Graeme. Bye bye,

Bon

AC/DC

PS. Graeme, if you can still manage the other $50 I'd love ya f'rever. It's no fun waitin' round to be a millionaire!!!

I got a letter from Bon in May, when AC/DC landed in Sydney. The Youngs had gone back to their Mum's place in Burwood but Bon was staying in a motel near Bondi Beach. They were in town for gigs but his voice had given out, so instead they went into the studio at Alberts to record some new material. The letter was pretty typical stuff from Bon, except the one paragraph when he told me he missed me. It was nice to hear that from him every now and again; he liked to sneak it in amongst the everyday banter. Bon knew that I knew him better than anyone and I think he missed that comfort. He knew he could trust me. I was important to him, and in a quiet moment he wanted to let me know. It didn't mean much, but it meant a lot to me. I missed him too, sometimes.

The problem was that what Bon said to me and what he said to the media were two different things. The RAM article he mentioned in his letter was all about this hot new punk band, AC/DC, and their outrageous lead singer. It was about how Bon had cut loose from Fraternity and found musicians that appreciated his filthy sense of humour. It was very light-hearted, for the most part. The RAM interviewer was a little taken aback when Bon said he'd left his wife to join AC/DC.

'I dug the band more than I dug the chick so I joined the band and left her,' he bragged.

I was absolutely stunned when I read it. It was really fuck-ing hurtful - why would he want me to read something like that? The next time he called me at work I unloaded both barrels on him.

'How could you bloody say that?' I exploded. 'And in an interview! You're a real bastard.'

'What the hell are you talking about?'

'*I dug the band more than I dug the chick.*'

'Oh, Christ,' he sighed. He told me he didn't mean it, he was just kidding around and it was taken out of context. 'You know what the media is like,' he said.

I knew what Bon was like. He was always playing up to this rock star image, trying to be controversial and provoke a reaction. He didn't mean half the shit he said, but it really hurt my feelings. I was so embarrassed.

'I'm really sorry, 'Rene,' he told me. 'You know I love ya.'

'I don't give a shit,' I told him, scanning over the article again. 'And what's this crap about you getting your ear pierced on a crayfishing boat? You got your ear pierced in a beauty salon in Adelaide a week after my twenty-first birthday.'

Bon didn't say anything, he just started laughing. *What a bullshit artist*, I thought.

May 20 1975
Irene Scott
2 Franklin St Henley Beach South Australia

 From:
1 Spring St Melbourne Victoria

 (Letter included 2 torn out pages from a BC comic book)

 Part II

 This is a sample of ole BC. I'd have to enclose the whole book but this will 'ave ta do mate. The books ain't mine (tut tut).

 Hope all is good.

 Bon

AC/DC were starting to build a following. It wasn't the same endless rounds of pub and club gigs; with their single climbing the chart, they were booking higher profile shows. Back in Melbourne, they played high-energy sets filled with tunes from High Voltage and a bunch of cover songs; Chuck Berry, The Stones and Elvis. They played sixth on the bill at the Concert for Bangladesh at the Myer Music Bowl and blew Daddy Cool off the stage. In May, they play back-to-back shows at the Hard Rock Café for Schoolkids Week that were total hysteria. They supported Richard Clapton at the same venue shortly afterwards. In June, they played with Split Enz and Skyhooks at Festival Hall. (Skyhooks were massive by that point. Split Enz were new and the audience didn't get it; they were booed off the stage. During AC/DC's set, Bon attempted to swing over the seats at Festival Hall wearing a Tarzan outfit and accidentally landed in the middle of the crowd, where mad AC/DC fans ripped off his loincloth. He had to play the rest of the gig in his undies.) On June 16, AC/DC returned to Festival Hall to play their first headline show at the venue, supported by Stevie Wright and John Paul Young, and Michael Browning arranged to have the gig filmed. His sister Coral was working in the music industry over in London and she was talking up the band to anyone who would listen. Browning wanted the band overseas as quickly as possible.

June 11, 1975

To:
Irene Scott
16 York St Prospect S.A.

From:
59A Wellington St St Kilda VIC

Dear Rene,

How are they hangin. This is just a shorty to let you know I'll be in Adelaide on June 9th for a couple of weeks so if your still speakin to me I'll be around for tea as often as possible. Are you still going to have a do with Cath and Barry. I got a letter from Cath the other day – really good. I think she likes me.

Graeme is in Melb & has come along to a couple of gigs & ended up on his knees worshipping our shit house. We're in Ballarat tonight – I think he's hitching down when he finishes work tonight. He's my favourite earthling for sure. Ralph offered him a job the other night. He might do it after his Europe tour. Don't know for sure. He's giving me his bike when I'm in Adelaide & that should be a buzz (man). His scar's a beaut. A bit of competition. I'm glad that's all he got though.

Told me that (confidential) uncle (of Frat fame) with his new band "Warm Hammer" is going to blow us off the stage at some Adelaide gig. Wish him luck for me.

We're doing Festival Hall on Monday (Queen's Birth) – it's our own show. It's being filmed and all for promotion films overseas for our new single "High Voltage Rock 'N' Roll". The single will also be on the High Oct album replacing one of the more shit house things. Probably LT Lover.

High Voltage (LP) has made a gold album (last week) so it caused a slight celebration. I'm going to give it to mum so I told her to make a space on her mantelpiece. She told me to write some clean songs for the next one but…wait till you hear a couple of em. One's called "She's Got the Jack" & it's already been recorded. Sounds good.

The band is nothin like it was when you heard it last. Got a couple of better players, better equipment & songs, just better all round. So watch out. We'd be the best band in Aus as long as you don't want your poofta shit (e.g. Cunthooks). Still I guess that's of no interest to you. Big headed bastard I know…but still lovable.

Give my love and regards to all who deserve it. See you in a couple of weeks.

Bon X

PS. Graeme just turned up with a joint. Goodnight. Says G'day ay-Fay. So does me!!!

The way Bon talked about AC/DC was similar in some ways to the way he had spoken about Fraternity, but it had a different meaning to me than it had previously. I wasn't part of it anymore. It wasn't my struggle. *Good on you if it's going to happen*, I thought, but I wasn't really invested in it. I was no longer part of Bon's dream.

It was interesting that he had heard about Chisel because they weren't on anyone's radar back in 1975. In the constant musical chairs of the Adelaide music scene, Uncle ended up joining Cold Chisel (or 'Warm Hammer', as Bon dubbed them) and Jim Barnes briefly left the band to go and sing with Fraternity. Jim asked me my opinion before he went and I gave him some really bad advice.

'Fraternity are already established,' I told him. 'It would be a really good move for you.'

Cold Chisel had a brilliant future ahead, but at that point they were still finding their feet. They played a lot of covers, everything from 'Georgia' to Deep Purple (because Ian was a huge fan of Ritchie Blackmore). Those guys were ambitious and extremely clever but they didn't take themselves too seriously. Aside from Jim and Steve Prestwich (who had some issues because Jim was a Scot and Steve was from Liverpool), they were all very calm. I never heard the members of Cold Chisel criticise each other the way the guys in Fraternity had done.

Bon met Ian for the first time when he came to Adelaide in June. I hadn't planned it, Bon just turned up at the house one day with a box of booze in his arms and Ian was sitting on the couch with a guitar in his hands.

'G'day,' Bon said, sizing him up.

Ian said hello in his quiet voice, then played a few bars of 'Baby, Please Don't Go'. Bon smiled and Ian smiled back, and that was that. I didn't actually tell Bon that Ian and I were seeing each other, but he figured it out fast enough. Ian knew that Bon was my ex but it didn't really seem to bother him. Nothing really did.

Later that week, Bon brought Angus round so I could make him a curry. Bon wanted the London special, which meant something to burn the roof off your mouth. Poor Angus didn't know what hit him; he sat at my kitchen table saying 'fuck me' over and over, coughing and spluttering, downing glass after glass of water. I don't know if Angus had much of a palette back then. It was a bit of a step up from a pie and sauce.

AC/DC released a new single called 'High Voltage' at the end of June. It wasn't on the High Voltage album; the guys just decided they liked the title so they wrote a song with the same name. It was an absolute firecracker, too. It had these spiky guitars and an unforgettable chorus; it was the first song they put out that made you want to pump your fist in the air (not that I did much of that myself). The lyrics were pure Bon, all about being a rock 'n' roll rebel. Even before the record came out, they'd play it at a gig and people would sing along after the first chorus. I knew the second I heard it that it was going to be a hit. I liked the video, too. It was footage from the Festival Hall show in June, with AC/DC up in lights, the whole band stomping around the stage and the audience just going nuts. When I saw it on Countdown I was relieved that Bon was out of the dress. *That's more like it*, I thought. *Straight up rock 'n' roll!*

By mid-1975 everyone watched Countdown, every Sunday night. Molly Meldrum seemed to love everything, regardless of whether or not it was shit, which annoyed me a bit, but Countdown was where you saw all the latest Aussie bands playing all the latest songs, and if you were into music you didn't want to miss it. It seemed like AC/DC was on the show every second week, and half the time they came out in ridiculous costumes, like the time they put Angus in a gorilla suit and Bon came out as Tarzan, or the time they dressed Angus as a schoolboy superhero. The kids loved it, but I couldn't take them seriously when they did things like that. I thought the circus distracted people from the incredible music they were making. I just didn't *get* it.

I was glad to see that Bon was having fun. He told me he felt like the band made room for him; like the whole thing adjusted to fit his shape. It was a really different experience for him. The Valentines were just ridiculous; I don't think anyone really took them seriously, and Fraternity took everything way too seriously. If those guys were having fun, you didn't see it in their performances. They always seemed to be pissed off with each other. I drew a cartoon in London of Bruce yelling at John the drummer, with a caption that read 'Faster fuck you, JF!', which summed up their attitude pretty well. It was all very heavy with those guys. With AC/DC, Bon could do whatever he wanted. He was free to work it out as he went along. It's not like I saw him on television and thought, *That's the real Bon!*, but he was headed in the right direction. A big part of his personality was coming through.

The High Voltage album got a big bump when the 'High Voltage' single was released; they sold 125,000 copies of the record all up, and 50,000 of that was after the single was released. I didn't know if Bon was making money. He seemed to be asking Graeme for money a lot, but as long as he was making payments to Custom Credit, it was none of my business.

Shortly after he came to Adelaide, the band relocated from Melbourne to Sydney and Bon moved back into the Squire Inn at Bondi Junction. Around the corner in Ebley Street there was a venue called The Bondi Lifesaver, which was Sydney's answer to the Largs Pier Hotel. It was knocked together from the shells of a couple of townhouses, with high walls out the front and a fishtank at the back of the room, and hundreds of sweaty music fans crammed inside, listening to the best bands Australia had to offer. When they landed in Sydney, The Lifesaver (or 'Wifeswapper', as some called it) became Bon's second home. AC/DC played there regularly and Bon drank there when they didn't. There were plenty of women around and he had plenty of fun; Bon's exploits with the ladies were the stuff of legend in the band. But he and I didn't talk about it, not back then. He didn't want to tell me and I wasn't interested.

In July, AC/DC went back into the studio at Alberts. They had a few tracks from the recording sessions Bon had mentioned back in April, but they wanted enough material for a whole new album - something stronger than the first, an album as good as the 'High Voltage' single. Malcolm and Angus wrote the music with George, testing out the tracks on the piano before they played them on guitar. Bon supplied the lyrics. He told me it was the best stuff he'd ever done.

'Maybe you could do the album cover,' Bon said.

He wanted me to draw a cartoon of AC/DC flying out through the roof of a high school. I drew a picture of Bon instead, with lightning coming out of his crotch.

When they finished recording, the band went back to Melbourne. They were booked in to play a series of free shows in the Miss Myer section of the Myer department store during the school holidays, but they didn't make it past the first gig. Thousands of screaming fans turned up and stormed the stage. Girls fainted, gear went flying and the band had to hide in the change rooms. Bon was left behind and dozens of rabid teenage girls tore his clothes off - jeans and everything. I'm sure he loved it.

AC/DC were getting this reputation as a really filthy, out-of-control rock act but they had a huge following of teenage girls, which I think had a lot to do with their Countdown appearances. Their management played it to the hilt. Back in Sydney, Alberts put together an advertising campaign for 2SM in which a Mum rants and raves about 'disgusting' AC/DC.

'AC/DC - they're not a nice band!' the ad finished.

Anything to sell records.

Bon was gargling port before the gigs to make his voice hoarse and Angus had started climbing on to his shoulders during the show. Everywhere they played, there was chaos. Bon thought it was a laugh. If it made Mums and Dads nervous, well that was just fantastic.

The guys were back in Melbourne by September, staying at the Freeway Gardens Motel. That's the place, according to AC/DC legend, that Bon slept with a massive girl by the name of Rosie before writing a song about her. AC/DC was overrun by groupies, and sleeping with them had become some kind of Olympic sport; Bon supposedly bedded three girls a day for four days straight at one point.

Up until then, I knew nothing about it. He didn't pretend to be a saint - he'd told me a few stories about his glory days with The Valentines and there was the odd comment here or there when he joined AC/DC, but it's not like he painted me a picture. Then one day I got a letter that unlocked the door and threw it wide open. Pat Pickett, the court jester who was always up at Hemming's Farm in the Fraternity days, had gone to Melbourne to join the AC/DC entourage. He dove headfirst into whatever insanity was going on over there and Bon decided to send me a report. In the letter, he said that he and Pat Pickett had had a couple of groupies back at their hotel, In the letter, he said that he and Pat picket had a couple of groupies back at their hotel and Pat had done something really gross to one of them. I don't want to repeat the story. I didn't understand why he thought I would find it funny. I couldn't understand why he found it funny.

I didn't say anything to him about it, but I thought it was a real low point. He'd had a bit of success, and all of a sudden he thought he was entitled to do anything to anyone; the band was so popular and so many girls were throwing themselves at him that it had totally messed up his idea of reality. I was really disgusted with him. I tore up the letter and threw it away. The only thing I kept was his signature at the bottom of the page.

Bon X, he signed off, *AC/DC*.

September 13, 1975
Sat. 7.30 P.M.

Good evening 'Rene,

How's everything spunk, all's well i trust. Got a few hours before we start work tonight so we're having a quiet time watching T.V. with a couple of bottles & a bag of dope. We don't start till 1.00am Sun at the Hard Rock Cafe.

Have you been on holiday yet. You said you were going to Sydney I think, great place. I was up there for a couple of weeks just recently & I was thinking you'd really dig the place. Adelaides allright to be buried in but not for one so young & spunky (unless your looking for a husband?) Saw Mick & Carol while I was there & they had me & Ralph round for tea & a get drunk rage. They're both really happy ecept mick would dig to get a band. Hes play'd a couple of night club gigs but left cause he had to wear suits & tie & turn down etc. They both have good jobs & live in a good enough flat & have a motor bike each & go camping (tents) on weekends in the bush & thats about that but it was still good to see them again. But Sydneys a fun place so take Faye & go stay there for a while.
We'll be in Adelaide next week but thats all I know as yet. We'll be there 1 week so you can ask me for tea & drinks one night (we have two nights off I think so we'll get drunk) I'm not doing too bad on the booze thing these days & am getting drunk quite regularly. But I'm a peace full drunk now. Have I still got any friends in Adelaide? No cunt ever writes to me. Hows Graeme is he still hurt. Silly cunt. Hows the bike. Just as well it wasn't the Harley. I would have killed him.
How is the family. All well i hope.
Heard from Soooooo Choooo lately & is there still a band called Fraternity. Thats all the news mate & all the questions so i'll fuck off. Don't forget to buy some booze (burbon: jim beam) for my return (ta ta ta taaaaa!!!).
I'm off to roll a joint so ill see ya later.

Bon

When AC/DC came back through Adelaide in October, Ian and I had broken up. There wasn't much to it, he just wanted to focus on his music. There were no screaming arguments or long discussions, he just told me he needed a break and that was it. I didn't complain about it but I really missed him. I think I realised for the first time that Ian had been a bit of a crutch and that my life was a bit empty without him. I hadn't made any plans for myself, not for a long while.

Fay and I had moved out of Henley Beach and back to Mum's place in Prospect, where Bon came to visit me the next time the band came through on tour. I was feeling pretty miserable. I told him I was thinking about moving interstate. Sydney sounded good, or maybe Melbourne. Bon thought it was a great idea; he told me Adelaide was no place to die, then he launched into a speech about The Bondi Lifesaver and all the amazing gigs AC/DC had played there, and all the other bands he had seen. He really liked The Keystone Angels (soon to become The Angels and sign with Alberts).

Bon was pretty full of himself. I wasn't really involved in the conversation, but he didn't really notice. He also didn't stay long. He said he was heading off to a party, which made me feel even worse. If there was a party in Adelaide and Bon was going, Ian and the Chisel guys would probably be there too.

Meanwhile, Fay and Graeme were also in trouble. Graeme had been feeling restless and decided it was time to end the relationship, but changed his mind a couple of days later and came looking for Fay to apologise. He found her asleep in front of the heater, bathed in sweat. Instead of reconciling with her, he launched into a lecture about how she would burn the house down and die in the fire. When he finished ranting, he asked if the two of them could still go to England in October, as they had planned. Fay was totally overwhelmed - she said it was a good time for a break. Graeme went to lick his wounds in Bangkok and Fay went off to England for a five-week holiday.

Fay ran into Bon at the airport on the day she was flying out. AC/DC had just finished a week of gigs in Adelaide and they were both headed to Melbourne on the same flight. Bon saw a few familiar faces in Fay's farewell party.

'I thought they were all here for me,' he laughed.

As they boarded the plane, Angus and Bon loaded Fay up with their old Penthouse and Playboy magazines.

'Something to read on the flight,' Bon winked.

Fay took them, she said, because it seemed rude not to.

When Fay got back from London, she started seeing Don Walker. I didn't blame her, he was pretty suave. The problem was Graeme, who came back to Adelaide wanting to patch things up. He got wind of her new romance as soon he flew in and fireworks ensued. Graeme found Fay at the Largs Pier watching a Cold Chisel gig and he started yelling at her, right in the middle of the bar. It was completely out of character for him. Graeme told Fay he had gifts for her, and if she didn't come with him straight away their relationship was over (or at least that was the gist of it). Fay wasn't really one to make a scene so she agreed to go.

Graeme was always incredibly generous. He gave Fay a beautiful hand-beaded silk dress from Bangkok and lots of other little gifts. She was grateful, but secretly she was very confused. Graeme had thought about things while he was away and decided that he wanted to get married, whereas Fay had decided it was definitely over. When he proposed to her, she had no idea what to say.

Before Fay knew what was happening, Graeme had phoned Isa in Perth. She spoke to her son for a long while before Graeme handed Fay the phone.

'Don't marry my son,' Isa told her. 'Having one of you girls on my conscience is bad enough. I don't want another.'

November XX, 1975

Dear Rene,

What a cunt of a night. Just got back from Canberra a day early & no one is expecting us until tomorrow. Got no booze, no dope & nobody except my own to play with. Shit. & to top it off I left my black (green) book in the bus, which broke down in Canberra. Hope your night is better.

Played in ACT this week. A couple of pub jobs & one high scholl dance (to over 1000 kids). Don't think you've heard but we did a Festival Hall concert on Cup Day (Tues last) to about 5000 & she was a beaut. Shows that size are the only ones I really like. Melb pubs (a la Largs Peer) give us all the shits but help pay the rent. Start the Q/land tour next week & all I got to say about that one is Q/land…look out! I think the promoter is gonna call the tour: "The AC/DC Lock Up Your Daughters Show" or something along those lines. Can't understand why. Hmmmm.

Finished the new album at long last. The H.V. album is still in the charts but slowly dropping out. Still it's been there for about 18 weeks. I reckon after the Brisbane tour it'll sell enough records to give us three gold albums. The record is the highest selling L.P. Alberts Music has ever had. Sold over 40,000 & gold (3rd) is 45,000. So I'll be able to paper a wall with little trophys. The next album wil tell. I reckon we'd have to be the hottest band in the country at the moment, not bad for a 29-year old 3rd time round has been.

AMCO jeans are gonna do a big promotion thing with us soon. At least I think it's AMCO. & as part of the deal they're giving the band two weeks in Bali. Air fares – the whole bit. We'll do that early Jan before going to Eng. Then we'll be doing a tour supporting, possibly, ZZ Top. It's not definite yet so don't say nothing ok. I think we're playing Adelaide

University on New Year's Eve. I guess they'd be advertising it by now wouldn't they?

Has Love & Rowell & Roves (??) given birth to their result of a fuck yet? If you see 'em say g'day for me & wish em well. & The Fraterns. How are they.

I'm going through a fucking funny period at the moment. Hope you don't mind a heart balm letter. Don't wanna settle with anybody else because I'm always on the road & won't be here long & on the other hand there's 20-30 chicks a day I can have the choice of fucking but I can't stand that either. Mixed up.

I like to be touring all the time just to keep my mind off personal happenings. Become a drunkard again & I can't go through a day without a smoke of hippy stuff. I just wanna get a lot of money soon so I can at least change a few little things about myself. (More booze & dope. Not really.) I just wanna be famous I guess. Just so when people talk about ya it's good things they say, that's all I want. But right now I'm just lonely. I've got a million things I'd like to write about right now but I just can't be fucked (jet lag I think).

Heard from Faye yet or brother Graeme. I guess he'll still be at sea. Tell him, if you can, that we leave for our tour next week but don't know what day as yet, ok. He said he'd come for a run with us. I'm gonna have him working for me one of these days. I like that kid (even though he's a fuckin hippy).

You'll never guess what I did in Canberra…I went on a guided tour (with about 100 people) of Parliment House & all the govt places such as the war memorial, which was fantasso. Phil the drummer was with me & we were stoned, of course. Got some photos took outside govt house & then we went to Whitlams house & took some there too. Had a rave to the guards on the gates of his mansion & I'm sure they thought we were mad but we were just a couple of tourists out for the day.

Are you still coming to Melbourne. Look if you can't make up your mind what to do I know some great people in Sydney & if maybe you wanted to go there I can help you get started.

Say hello to mum for me. Hope your getting on, but can't see it. Did Barry & Cath get my letter? Hope so.

I sent custom credit $150 & told them to stay off the back for a few months. They sent me a balance sheet & I only owe them $187 so I'm gonna send em that out of the next couple of weeks pay. I'll have to get in & see Rowell soon too. He must think I've vanished off the face of the earth but you know what I'm like.

Hay has our D.I.V.O.R.C.E. happened yet. Do I get a bit of paper or what. I don't care if I never get a D cause I'm not planning on marrying again unless she's a millionaire & I think my chances of finding one are scarce. But when I pull out my photo album I like sayin "& this is my wife." They all fancy you & tell me what taste in spunk I've got.

Well 'Rene I could rave for hours; it's already a fuckin novel. Hey, pssst, wake up. Sorry but I felt terrible when I started writing & I feel better now. Think I'll borrow a "stick book" from Picket and go to bed. Can't see much else happening. Look after yerself & write soon ok?

Bon X

PS. Heard a rumour that the Nobels (Bob roadie Nobel) were coming to live in Melb. Maybe......just a thought. See ya.

I had joked with Bon about getting a divorce, but I didn't really see the need. It just wasn't important to me. When he raised it in his letter it made me feel odd, but I think it was the context. Bon sounded terrible.

What a cunt of a night. It wasn't like him to feel that sorry for himself, even if he had run out of beer. I thought he must have been kidding around, because after that it was all good news with the band - gold records, commercial deals, amazing opportunities. It all sounded fantastic. But the letter rambled on and on, and he repeated a lot of things he'd already told me, until eventually he managed to say what he was trying to say. He snuck it in where he thought it wouldn't be noticed; *I'm just lonely.*

It broke my heart to read that line. I knew it was just for a minute, just in that moment when Bon was alone with a pen in his hand, but he would never have written it without a really heavy heart. I knew how much it took for Bon to open up like that. And I knew he was reaching out to me because he didn't have anyone else. Everyone loved him, but no one really knew him the way I did. Canberra, Parliament House, his excellent taste in spunk and Pat Pickett's porno mag - that was just Bon covering his tracks. He couldn't let such a sad thought hang out there in the breeze.

I've got a million things I'd like to write, he said. I never found out what he meant. Maybe he had things to say to me about our relationship, or maybe he just wanted to tell me stories about life on the road. I don't know. And I was too sad to ask.

In the end, Bon chose the band. His letter was just a moment of weakness, and even in that moment, most of his thoughts were about his career. That's what he was, a rock 'n' roll singer. Even if it made him unhappy, that's what he would always be.

CHAPTER 8

Ian and I were seeing each other again by December, but it was only temporary. I re-applied for a transfer to Melbourne and Cold Chisel had their own plans to move interstate, possibly Sydney. We enjoyed it while we could.

On New Year's Eve, I saw AC/DC play at Football Park in West Lakes. Cold Chisel was on the bill along with Fraternity, but Bon and his band really stole the show. AC/DC had just released their second album and it was a total shift of gears, a little whack of dynamite called T.N.T. They still had that rhythm and blues swing, but there were a few tunes on the record that just blew you away, including the title track. It was right up there with 'High Voltage'; the minute you listened to it you couldn't get it out of your head. There were a few gems on the album, although I tried not to pay too much attention to the lyrics. If I thought too hard about all the macho bullshit, I couldn't take them seriously, and some of it was just gross. Bon was particularly proud of 'The Jack', a smutty double entendre about playing cards and venereal disease, but I thought it was a bit obvious. Who wants to hear about Bon's brush with STDs? I had no idea what he was getting up to with women and I had a strong feeling I didn't want to know, but AC/DC fans weren't nearly as squeamish. They loved all the sex and smut; they couldn't get enough of it. The band sent T.N.T. out to the media wrapped in ladies' underwear and the album sold 11,000 copies in its first week.

The gig at Football Park was a circus, which according to Bon was just the average scene at an AC/DC show at that point. The band arrived late and only made it through two songs before the venue cut their power. Out of nowhere, Bon appeared with a set of bagpipes, riding through the crowd on somebody's shoulders and making the most god-awful noise while the audience hollered and clapped their hands. I didn't think Bon knew how to play bagpipes (and I was right, he sounded terrible). It was all part of the show. Bon was being his over-the-top self and the crowd loved him for it.

After the gig, Bon invited us back to the hotel room along with a few of his old Adelaide friends. It was all very casual, no rock 'n' roll excess. I was in a white dress with a big split up the side and platform shoes that made me look about nineteen feet tall. I had built up a fair tan from all my days down at the beach, which was a bit of an achievement. The last time I tried to get a bit of colour, Bon spent the night laughing at me while he rubbed moisturiser into my horrible red sunburn. At the hotel, he looked me up and down with his eyebrows raised.

'She never looked like that when I was with her,' he told Ian.

I think he was trying to be nice.

Bon told us that AC/DC had done a deal with Atlantic Records in the UK; they were heading over in the new year to start touring. I got the impression that he wanted me to be proud of him, but it's not like he was bragging. It was all very matter-of-fact. The thing that struck me whenever Bon talked about AC/DC was that they made plans and then they followed through with them. Everything was very clearly mapped out and virtually everything he talked about turned out to be true. I just felt like he wanted me to know that things were different for him this time round. He didn't really need to tell me, it was pretty bloody obvious. I'd heard more people talking about AC/DC in the last month than I'd heard in three whole years with Fraternity. They were obviously doing well.

I was extremely happy for Bon, but I didn't feel like I wanted to be a part of his success. If anything, I felt like it drew a line under the relationship. He and I had gone down different paths and his life and mine were no longer connected. That was fine by me, I was still very young. I had big hopes for my own future.

I had spent a whole year in Adelaide just decompressing from the marriage. It was an easy place to be. There was never a lot of money in the bank, but I could pay my rent and buy beer on the weekend and I had enjoyed myself with Ian. There wasn't much to it. In the back of my mind, I had the sense that I would move on at some point. It was just a matter of when.

As time passed, Adelaide contracted around me. Vince and Helen had just had a baby so their hands were full and they had less time to spend with friends, Cold Chisel were preparing to go, and I was back at Mum's (which, as much as I loved her, was a bit depressing). I was restless. I wanted to throw myself into something completely different, the way I had when I was nineteen. I just didn't know what. I didn't have Bon's vision. I didn't know what I wanted out of life, but I figured I'd have a better chance of figuring it out in a different city.

I moved to Melbourne in January 1976. Fay had an old school friend named John who was living in the eastern suburbs, in Surrey Hills, and he offered to put me up until I got settled. I landed on his doorstep right after New Year, with one suitcase and no clue what I was doing. Melbourne had seemed like a better option than Sydney because I had friends that travelled there from Adelaide all the time and I'd been there once myself, when Andrea and I flew over for her cousin's wedding. (We spent virtually the whole weekend in the hotel.) When I moved, I realised that the city was a total mystery to me, that I didn't know anyone and I didn't know my way around. Bon was in Melbourne, but I didn't want to call him the day after I landed - it seemed a bit desperate. I figured I'd give it a week or two before letting him know his wife was in town.

John lived in pleasant weatherboard in a leafy suburban street with his girlfriend Sonia and his flatmate Melvin. It was a peaceful place but really isolated, much farther from the city centre than I'd been at home. Getting to work was a trek - two trams in and two trams out every day - but I was glad I worked in the city at least. The heart of Melbourne was incredible. I got a rush when I stepped off the tram in Bourke Street and felt the high-rise buildings crowding around me. There was a height limit on buildings in Adelaide, for reasons I never quite understood, so it didn't look or feel like a real city. Melbourne buildings had *ambition*. It wasn't quite London, but it would do.

John was incredibly hospitable but Sonia didn't love having me around, at least that's the impression she gave. She snapped open the newspaper the day after I arrived and started scanning through the real-estate section, and did the same every day afterwards, trying to find me a flat. Melvin was really nice. He was a skinny bloke with a bland kind of face; a bit of a nerd, but kind. He hung out with me once or twice and I was grateful for the company.

Melvin came with me to the Burvale Hotel on Springvale Road to see AC/DC one night. I don't know if he was interested in the band or interested in me, but I was glad he came. I was really nervous about seeing Bon, I'm not sure why. I guess I was on unfamiliar ground, without my usual gang of friends around me, whereas Bon was in his element - the centre of attention. I hadn't told him I was in town and I didn't know what kind of reception I would get (though as it turned out, I wasn't the one who should have been worried).

At the end of AC/DC's set I went up to say hello, dragging my poor housemate behind me.

'This is Melvin,' I said, introducing him to Bon.

'Melvin?!' Bon roared. '*Melvin?!*'

He laughed like it was the worst name he'd ever heard and pulled me over to one side to have a word.

'Don't just go out with anyone, 'Rene,' he said.

Melvin was still well within earshot and Bon wasn't trying to be subtle. He had stepped off the stage full of macho bullshit and decided to wave a big red flag in my face, just because he was on home turf and just because he could. *How bloody rude*, I thought, though I was secretly pretty amused. Melvin didn't react at all. He was probably used to that sort of thing.

Bon called me a few days later and invited me to lunch.

'C'mon spunk,' he said. 'Let me take you out.'

He said he'd pick me up out front of work the next day. I was working on Domain Road in South Yarra and Bon said there was a great new bistro he wanted to show me, just round the corner. *Bistro?!* I thought, but OK.

He was in a fantastic mood when he arrived. As we walked down the street, Bon belted out the words to AC/DC's latest single, 'It's a Long Way to the Top (If You Wanna Rock 'n' Roll)', only he changed the lyrics.

'It's a long way to the *shop* if you want a *sausage roll*.'

It was the first time I ever heard it and I was doubled over laughing. (The effect wears off over time.) 'It's a Long Way to the Top' was all over the radio by that point. It was AC/DC's highest-charting single - they'd finally cracked the Top 10 - and it was all about Bon's life. It was about being broke and half-starving in the back of a tour bus with The Valentines; it was about smoking dope with Fraternity and playing to empty rooms in nothing-and-nowhere English towns; it was about getting old and going grey, and risking everything to chase a dream. The song was an instant anthem that connected with a huge audience, but I knew the minute I heard it that it was something deeply personal for Bon. Not that he was really *feeling* it that day. He was just trying to make me smile.

The bistro he wanted to take me to was chock-a-block when we arrived; they didn't have a spare table. Bon was at a bit of a loss, so we wandered up Toorak Road and decided to eat at the next place we found.

'There you go,' Bon said. '*Eduards*.'

'Ah yes, *Eduards*,' I repeated, in my poshest accent.

Eduards was a fancy French restaurant with absolutely nobody inside. It looked like a fine dining place and we didn't look like fine diners. I was in my work clothes, which were conservative enough, but typical Bon was in ball-hugging jeans and a skin-tight band T-shirt.

'G'day,' he said to the guy on the door, flashing him a toothless smile.

I don't think they were used to having customers like Bon, but it's not like they had much of a choice. It was us or no one. We were served by a waiter who had one hand behind his back and a white napkin over his arm. It was a first for us, eating at an expensive restaurant, but Bon acted like he owned the place. He was never intimidated. He also paid the bill, which was just bizarre. It's the first time we'd been out where I didn't hear, *Got five bucks 'Rene?* or find Bon crouched over my purse, digging for spare change.

We talked about people back home and he asked about my family, and he told me about AC/DC's new, improved plans. They were still heading to England, but they'd be going to Sydney first to finish their new album.

'Jesus, another one?' I laughed.

He just shrugged. They'd be away for a while and they didn't know when they'd be able to get back into the studio.

Before he dropped me back at work, I got the courage to ask Bon if there was anyone in Melbourne he could introduce me too. I was pretty desperate for friends.

'Uh, yeah,' he chuckled, with a funny little look on his face. 'There's a chick called Mary. I reckon the two of you would get along.'

I loved Melbourne. It was the kind of place I could get lost in and then find myself again, and it was a real music city. This was the era when Skyhooks, Ted Mulry Gang, Sherbet and Billy Thorpe were filling concert halls, but dozens of other groups were playing down at the local. It was the birth of Australian pub rock. AC/DC were right out front of the pack, but you could tell something was building up behind them, with bands like The Ferrets and Jo Jo Zep and The Falcons building their own small following and a dozen big Aussie bands like Chisel, who were waiting in the wings. In Melbourne, you could go out and see great live music every week, Thursday through Saturday nights. You could go to the pub on Sundays too, but your beer came with a side of cocktail frankfurts and a dollop of mashed potatoes, and there weren't usually any bands playing.

There was so much to do, I just needed a few more friends to do it with. I had met a guy in Adelaide by the name of Richard Parr and he told me to look him up when I was in town, so I gave him a call towards the end of January. He was a roadie for a well-known country- rock act called The Dingoes. I didn't know him well but I figured he'd be into music. Richard was a very talkative bloke, very friendly, and he was nice enough to take me to a barbecue and introduce me to some of his friends. One of them was Maggie Tolhurst, wife of The Dingoes' guitarist Kerryn Tolhurst. Maggie was a wry, quietly-spoken woman with a six-year-old daughter and a huge love of music; we hit it off straight away. We swapped numbers and arranged to catch up again. Meanwhile, Vince Lovegrove had put me in touch with his little sister, Sue. Sue was just like her brother; she could make you laugh with just the expression on her face. I'd met her in Adelaide and I really liked her. She must have liked me too because we decided to move in together. Sue left her tiny bedsit on Inkerman Street and I left paper-snapping Sonia in Surrey Hills, and we moved into a house on Tennyson Road in Elwood. It was south of the city, not too far from the old AC/DC place in Lansdowne Street and not too far from the beach.

I made contact with Bon's friend Mary just after I saw him. They had a long history, which is why he was nervous about introducing us. I'd been married to him four years and he'd barely mentioned her name. They met in 1968 at a club called Tenth Avenue, when Bon was in The Valentines. He told her he liked her hippy beads and asked her to make him a set, and Mary had become a friend and a big fan of his band. She was a lovely person and Bon was incredibly fond of her.

Mary had dark hair, dark eyes and an easy laugh. She invited Sue and I round for drinks one night and introduced us to her friends, and later she and I went out for a drink. When it was just the two of us, smoking endless cigarettes over endless glasses of wine, the conversation naturally gravitated to the one thing we had in common - we talked a lot about Bon. Mary told me about Bon's adventures in The Valentines and I told her about Adelaide and London, and the disaster of our marriage. It was all very affectionate and very, very funny. It was nice to speak to someone who liked Bon as much as I did and knew him as something more than just a singer in a band.

Bon had told me that Mary was just a friend, but I guessed that she'd been more than a friend to him every once in a while. She never said it directly, but the way she spoke about him implied that they had been together, somewhere along the line. I didn't ask questions. By that stage I figured that half the girls I knew had slept with Bon at one point or another and it didn't bother me in the slightest. I was grateful to find another good friend so far from home.

Bon was recording in Sydney for most of February 1976, but AC/DC came back to Melbourne at the end of the month to shoot a new video for Countdown. The director had $400 bucks and a flatbed truck, and a really great idea. He wanted to load the band on to the tray and film them playing 'It's a Long Way to the Top' while the truck trundled through the centre of Melbourne. On February 23, the band, some fans and a bunch of bagpipe players gathered together and set off down Swanston Street, unknowingly creating a piece of Australian history. I saw it when everyone else did, on Countdown. Bon made me laugh, hamming it up for the camera and laughing while he sang.

What is that awful vest? I thought, and *why am I looking at Bon's naked stomach?* Mind you, you were hard-pressed to find a rock star with their shirt *on* in the Seventies. I don't recall seeing another rock star playing bagpipes though. There was Bon the mad Scotsman, honking into his pipes, and Rob Booth, Fraternity's old roadie and my old London flatmate, walking beside the truck. Towards the end of the film, I saw a female fan trying to give Bon her phone number and oh how I rolled my eyes. The clip was really fantastic, though. I'd never seen anything like it.

A few days after he shot the video, Bon called me at work and asked me to go out with him.

'We're having a party 'cause we've got about a dozen gold records,' he told me. 'I want you to come.'

Bon wasn't too far off - AC/DC had three plaques coming for the High Voltage album and three for T.N.T. The reception would be at a plush restaurant in the city called Lazars. They had the whole top floor booked for the presentation and half the Australian music industry would be there. Bon didn't tell me why he wanted *me* there and I didn't think to ask, but the minute I hung up the phone I started to feel uneasy. The more I thought about it, the worse I felt. I knew Bon wanted me to see how well he was doing, but I wasn't sure how he meant it. He was probably showing off. I didn't want to stand around all night like a spare tyre while people shook his hand and told him he was a legend. I remembered that night at the Pooraka when we first started going out, when Bon was swallowed up by his mates and admirers, and I was left watching from the sidelines. *No thanks*, I thought. I was far too proud for that. I got very anxious and I decided not to go.

I left a message for Bon at his hotel, but he either missed it or ignored it. He turned up on my doorstep on the night of the party and told me to get dressed.

'I'm not coming,' I said.

'Bullshit,' he replied. 'Get your clothes on.'

I mumbled a couple of weak objections but he wouldn't have a bar of it, so I gave up and headed for the bedroom. Bon sat on the end of the bed whistling and grinning while I found something decent to wear.

The party was in full swing when we arrived. There was a sea of people spread wall to wall at the venue and I recognised some of their faces from TV. I felt completely overwhelmed, heart in my throat, but Bon steered me through the crowd and began introducing me to people.

'This is my wife Irene,' he said.

Bon stayed close by for most of the night, but I was happy enough after a drink or three - in fact it turned out to be a really excellent party. I met Mark Evans' Mum and ended up on the dance floor with the notorious Pat Pickett, though I was spared his famous 'dance of the flaming arsehole'.

'He stuffs toilet paper down his arse, sets it on fire and runs out of the bar,' Bon laughed. He said it was very popular in Queensland.

Everything loosened up as the night wore on. Booze flowed freely and people laughed, and the band accepted their gold records without much ceremony. Bon gave me his plaque for High Voltage and told me to hang it on my wall.

'You can think of me when you look at it,' he winked.

At the end of the night, when we were all very merry, they wheeled a huge hollow cake into the middle of the room. A belly dancer popped out of its middle and Bon's eyes lit up. *Here we go*, I sighed.

'Hold me drink,' Bon said, and he was off like a shot, clambering up the side of the cake and attempting to dive into her cleavage.

'That'd be right,' I muttered with a smile.

Bon insisted on seeing me home in a taxi, and when we arrived at my place he asked if he could stay. We were drunk and happy, and it seemed like a good idea at the time. I didn't have a bedframe so we slept together on the floor.

Later, as Bon lay with his arms wrapped around me, he said, 'I still love you, 'Rene.'

Like a bitch, I laughed at him and turned away.

'That's all over,' I said.

I wasn't trying to hurt him. I wasn't angry or sad or disappointed anymore. And it's not that I didn't love him, I just didn't want to look like a fool. Bon might tell me he loved me in the middle of the night, but in the morning he would leave. And I didn't want him to think that I cared.

CHAPTER 9

AC/DC were headed back to Sydney in mid-March to play their final Australian shows before heading overseas. One of their last Melbourne gigs was at the Myer Music Bowl, supporting Little River Band, and it descended into chaos once again. The venue cut the power and the crowd rained beer cans on the stage in retaliation, booing Little River Band when they were brave enough to appear.

AC/DC were churning out hit songs like sausages and their fans were only getting rougher. The music had a lot to do with it - the farther along they went, the less rollicking rhythm and blues they played. Their sound got tougher and more macho with every tune - or at least that's how it sounded to me. 'T.N.T.' was released as a single in March, with its distinctive 'Oi Oi' chant, and it was like a battle cry for blokes with too much testosterone. It was a far cry from where they'd started out. When Bon first talked about joining the band, our friend Ron Alphabet had tried to talk him out of it because AC/DC was 'poofdah shit' in Ron's opinion. Boy, how things had changed.

I liked 'T.N.T.'. It was a great rock 'n' roll song that had a huge punch to it, and I was incredibly impressed with how well the guys were doing. The T.N.T. album was number two on the chart and High Voltage was still selling, and their songs seemed to be playing everywhere you went. I heard them in bars, at parties and on the radio, and on Countdown nearly every second week. You couldn't get away from them if you wanted to.

I think Bon was aware of it, but he didn't seem to care. He called me when he landed in Sydney, and all he could talk about was England. He just wanted to get on the plane and go. The whole AC/DC camp felt the same way - getting overseas was all that mattered, that was the plan all along. Michael Browning had taken the band on because he knew that they had international reach. George Young wanted his brothers to be bigger than The Easybeats. AC/DC had done well in Australia, but it wasn't nearly enough for them. It didn't mean anything if they didn't make it big around the world. And it wasn't even a question, they were just going to do it. They would start small and work hard and eventually they'd get to the top. That kind of focus didn't come naturally to Bon. He would never have gotten there on his own, but with Malcolm and Angus and the rest of them driving it, he just climbed on board and held on tight. He knew he was on to a good thing. He never said it, but he knew he was lucky.

AC/DC played their farewell gig at The Lifesaver on March 27, 1976. Angus flashed his arse at the crowd, apparently for the very first time. A woman decided to strip on stage and Bon hoisted her into the air over his head, while Angus mounted the bar and stomped his way from one end to the other. The floor shook and the fish tank shuddered, and the crowd had a bath in its own sweat. AC/DC went out with a bang and left the country without a glance over their shoulders.

Cold Chisel came through town in March, on their way back from gigs in Sydney. Ian brought me my old metal trunk filled with useful crap from Adelaide and stayed the night in Elwood before disappearing again. It was nice to see him as the guys in Melbourne weren't particularly impressive. I dated a bloke from work who was nice enough, but he had the social skills of a wombat. He had absolutely nothing to say. Sue began to whistle that 'Personality' tune under her voice whenever I brought him home, and that was the beginning of the end. I couldn't keep a straight face around him after that.

I decided to ignore men for a while and focus on music (because in my head they were two very separate things). Maggie Tolhurst took me under her wing and the two of us explored the live music venues of Melbourne together. There were suburban beer barns like the Matthew Flinders in Chadstone and the Prospect Hill in Camberwell, where Little River Band and Skyhooks would play every second weekend, but we preferred the smaller venues. The small clubs had sticky carpets and far more interesting bands. In the city, there was Bombay Bicycle Club and the Hard Rock Café; in Richmond there was the Kingston Hotel and the Tiger Room. We saw every group around back then; Lobby Loyde and The Coloured Balls, Dragon and Madder Lake. Cold Chisel settled in Melbourne for a few months after I moved there and I saw them a lot before they moved on to Sydney. We caught The Ferrets, Jo Jo Zep and Mondo Rock later on, plus dozens of bands whose names didn't live past the Seventies. If there was a gig on anywhere, Maggie and I would go.

There was a lot of talent in town, but my absolute favourite band was the one that Maggie's husband was in - The Dingoes. I was a huge fan and they had a big following. They'd had a minor hit in 1973 with a song called 'Way Out West', and they'd released a self-titled album in 1974, full of these beautiful, melodic, country-rock tunes. They were musicians' musicians, very well respected, but they'd hit a bit of a ceiling at home in Australia and they wanted to try their luck overseas. I met them just a few months before they left.

Late in March, I went to see them play at the London Tavern in Richmond and I sat at a table with some of The Dingoes' girlfriends and wives. Maggie stayed home that night, but she'd already introduced me to her husband Kerryn and the guitarist, Chris Stockley, along with Chris' wife Jenny. At the end of their set, the band came to join us and I was introduced to the rest of them, including a lovely guy by the name of John DuBois. John was The Dingoes' bass player and a really handsome bloke, with curly dark hair and a very gentle smile. He was softly spoken but he had plenty to say, and the two of us chatted easily as the evening wore on. At the end of the night, he asked me if I needed a lift home. When we climbed into the car, he asked if I wanted to go to his place for a drink. I said yes, very happily.

Mary was living quite close to John, so I walked over to her place in the morning, high heels in one hand, handbag in the other, and a slightly embarrassed smile on my face. She knew the band, of course.

'John Doo-BWAR!' she laughed. 'Tell me everything.'

That was the beginning of my brief relationship with John, who was a bit more age-appropriate than Ian but no less transient. The Dingoes would be in America by mid-year and our fling was just a stopover. It was lovely though; he was a really sweet man.

It honestly never occurred to me that there might be something odd about seeing three musicians in a row. I certainly didn't plan it. It's just that my friends and all of their friends were involved in the music industry and the music industry is full of musicians. It was just a weird coincidence that three guys I was involved with, to varying degrees, were each very important to Australian music. I had no idea it would turn out that way.

John and I were never really in a relationship, but we had a great time hanging out together. He was warm and intelligent and easy to be around, and his friends were all funny and talented. Maggie was shy but very wise, Kerryn Tolhurst was super smart and Jenny Stockley was incredibly bubbly. Richard Parr the roadie turned out to be a bit of a dill, but he had his charms - he came round to invite John and I out for a 'cup of chino' one morning and we were in stitches for the rest of the day.

Bon still wrote from England, but the letters were further apart and I didn't get nearly as many phone calls. I heard almost as much about Bon's life reading music magazines as I heard directly from him, and sometimes I couldn't remember where the stories had come from. The band was supposed to head out on tour with Back Street Crawler the minute they landed in London, but Back Street Crawler's guitarist (Paul Kossoff, ex-Free) had died a few weeks earlier. When they landed, their tour plans were in a shambles. Bon wrote an open letter to RAM saying 'that cunt Paul Kossoff fucked up our tour', but I'm sure he told me the same thing over the phone. It was around the same time he told me he'd been back to the Manor Cottage in Finchley, to say hi to the locals. Bon had great memories of the place but something had gone horribly wrong; not only did the clientele not recognise him, but he managed to walk into the middle of a bar fight and ended up getting glassed in the face.

'What do you mean you walked into a fight?' I asked. 'What happened?'

'Nothing happened!' he said. 'I walked in and opened my mouth to say hello and some bastard broke a fucking glass on my teeth.'

He was going to get a new set of dentures on Harley Street and he was pleased about that; he'd been missing teeth ever since the bike accident. (I didn't like his new smile, when I saw it. It looked totally unnatural, like it'd been painted into his mouth, although I guess it was better than the half-broken stumps he had before. I missed the smile Bon had when I met him, with a cute little chip in the front tooth.)

Just before he hung up the phone, Bon told me he'd run into an old friend from Adelaide.

'I saw Silver,' he said.

There was a slightly triumphant note to his voice, like he expected me to be shocked, but I had no idea who he was talking about.

'Who the hell is Silver?' I replied.

'Silver Smith,' he said. 'She was Margaret Smith back home. She lives in London now.'

I had a cold feeling in my stomach.

'Is her husband over there with her?' I asked.

'Nah,' Bon answered. 'That's all over now.'

That was all he needed to say; his cocky attitude told me the rest. The bizarre encounters I'd had with Margaret Smith back in Adelaide suddenly clicked into place and I realised that she had a history with Bon, and whatever had been between them was back on again. I felt like an idiot. It shouldn't have mattered by then, but Bon was no dummy. He was practically bragging about it. He wanted me to know about Silver, and for some reason I think he wanted it to hurt.

AC/DC's London debut was at the end of April at the Red Cow in Hammersmith. They played their first set to fifty-odd people and their second set to a packed room - legend has it that everyone who watched the first set ran out and called their friends during the break. The UK version of High Voltage was released at the end of the month, a compilation of tracks from the Australian High Voltage and T.N.T. albums, but the UK press didn't go crazy for it. The guys had champions in John Peel (who had been playing imported copies of their albums on the BBC) and Phil Sutcliffe (a journalist with Sounds magazine). The rest of the media was obsessed with the birth of punk and AC/DC didn't really fit the mould. But the band wasn't fazed, they just worked at it. They played club gigs around London throughout May, including a couple of shows at the legendary Marquee Club, which had hosted everyone from The Rolling Stones to The Yardbirds and Jimi Hendrix.

Whenever they spoke to the press, AC/DC did their best to ruffle feathers and make an impression, but it was their live shows that drew the grudging respect of the London music mafia. Angus flashed his arse at virtually every show, climbed up on Bon's shoulders and twitched when he played guitar like he was going into electric shock. They played loud and unapologetic rock 'n' roll, and once you saw them you couldn't forget them - they just needed to get enough eyes on their act. AC/DC set off on their first major UK tour in mid-June, the 'Lock

Up Your Daughters' tour, sponsored by Sounds magazine. They did nineteen gigs around Britain with varying success; sometimes they played to five people, sometimes the club was full, but everywhere they went they made new fans. The crowd in Glasgow went nuts for AC/DC and destroyed the venue, setting fire to the seats and taunting the security guards, cheering the band through three encores. (The venue sent a letter to the band, demanding payment for damages.) London was the final stop of the tour, a rowdy gig at the Lyceum where AC/DC staged a 'schoolgirl we'd most like to...' competition and awarded first prize to a leggy blonde in suspenders and a mini-dress. They knew how to make an impression.

Meanwhile back in Australia, they were making the wrong impression, at least in my opinion. The 'Jailbreak' single came out in June, along with a film clip they'd shot for Countdown before they left Australia. John and I sat on the couch watching it in amazement. It was just ridiculous. The cameraman must have been pissed; it looked like he was lying on the ground underneath Bon's crotch in some vain attempt to make Bon look taller, but all you got was an eyeful of his nuts. I don't know who came up with the whole Ned Kelly concept but everything about it was cheap, from the crappy explosions to the plastic guns to the weird arrows the guys had stuck all over their clothes. Angus didn't even bother to change out of his pyjamas for the shoot. It's not like we thought, *Wow! State-of-the-art!* It was corny and badly executed, even back then. The thing that bothered me most was that AC/DC were this amazing band but the clip was a joke. I thought they were underselling themselves. Of course, the rest of Australia disagreed. 'Jail-break' went to number 5, which was the band's highest-charting single yet. T.N.T. was selling three- or four-thousand copies a week and Alberts claimed that the total value of AC/DC sales had cleared a million dollars. I didn't know any of this at the time, I just thought Bon looked really terrible when you looked at him from his balls upward.

John DuBois and I were seeing each other for a few months before The Dingoes left for the States. It was winter when he took me out for our last dinner and dropped me off at my place with a goodbye hug. I didn't feel particularly sad that he was leaving, but it was a bad time of year to be saying goodbye to someone. Melbourne had become very cold and very grey all of a sudden.

Maggie stayed behind when the rest of the band left and she and I decided to live together. Sue wanted to get a flat with her new boyfriend, so the timing was perfect. I took the back room at Maggie's house in Lambeth Place in St Kilda and Maggie and her daughter shared a room towards the front. It was the first time I'd lived with a child since the Fraternity house in London and I was glad it was just the one - kids are pretty overwhelming when you're in your mid-twenties.

Maggie's Mum did a lot of babysitting so that Maggie and I could go out, and we certainly made the most of our freedom. Our favourite place at the time was the Station Hotel, a big old corner pub in Prahran. The guy who booked the bands would get up in front of the microphone every night, pissed as a newt, and tell everyone that the Station Hotel was where you came for 'no bullshit music'. It was a no-frills pub but it had a great atmosphere. The floorboards were covered in beer and cigarette butts, the punters were in work boots and denim jackets, and everyone was there to have a good time. Bands loved to play there. We'd seen The Dingoes there often enough, and Cold Chisel played the Station a lot when they were in town (with tunes that got better and better and a lead singer who got drunker and drunker as the band progressed). It was the kind of place that more established musicians would visit too, just because it was a great place to hang out and be seen. Maggie introduced me to a friend of hers at the bar one night who turned out to be "Bongo" Starkie from Skyhooks, although I didn't recognise him without the make-up.

When I wasn't seeing bands with Maggie I was over at Mary's place on the north side of the city. She and I had developed our own great friendship by then, but Bon still came up quite regularly. We'd read each other the letters he sent, most of which went into the rubbish shortly afterwards. The tone was pretty uniform; AC/DC were going great and everybody in England loved them.

'What does this say?' Mary asked me one day. 'He's kicking Oz?'

'Oz?' I said, examining the letter.

'Bon says he's kicking Oz,' she repeated.

'*Arse*, Mary. He's kicking arse,' I laughed.

'Isn't he always,' Mary smiled.

Mary had a letter from Bon after his 30th birthday in July, thanking her for remembering to send him a card. *Not many did*, he wrote. I sent Bon a card but I hadn't heard back from him. It had a cartoon drawing of legs sticking out from where the envelope was sealed and a speech bubble that said, 'I'm stuck.' He probably didn't reply because the joke was so bad - or possibly he was otherwise indisposed. I read RAM and Juke religiously and they were keeping a close eye on AC/DC's efforts overseas, so even when I didn't hear from Bon I heard from him. In an interview that came out about a month later, Bon said he'd fucked his birthday in, from 11.50pm until a quarter past midnight. AC/DC threw him a three-day party but the guest of honour never actually showed up.

After Bon's birthday on July 9, AC/DC played a gig at the Wimbledon Theatre that was broadcast as part of a Marc Bolan special, on a TV show called Superpop. Then they jumped on a plane and went to tour in Sweden, from where Bon claimed he sent me a postcard of a topless sunbather (I never received it). He also wrote a letter to the Melbourne Herald explaining that AC/DC were busy blowing polkas and oompah music out of the water (while enjoying the topless sunbathing).

At the end of July, the band went back to London and started a residency at the Marquee Club that in four weeks went from highly anticipated to absolute mayhem. They advertised the shows with a full-page photo of Angus, holding a letter from the city of Glasgow describing their gig as out of control. It worked a treat. The 700-capacity Marquee was filled with more than a thousand people each night, with TV crews turning up outside the venue to film the queue and journalists writing dazed reports about AC/DC's powerhouse live show. Phil Sutcliffe captured it beautifully in his article for Sounds:

...Phil Rudd's drums begin their relentless thump, Mark Evans' bass booms subliminally and the guitars of Angus and Malcolm Young strike a couple of hundred megaton chords. The volume is well-judged, bearable, no louder than, say, inside a rivet-gun. Angus starts to pace the stage, jack-knifing up and down over his guitar, already whipping jets of sweat and skeins of snot over the front rows...

The rhythms hit your heart like a trip-hammer and that's basic and essential but the reasons we are all inspired are the maniac onward rush of inventive, fluent solos from Angus (goddamn, amid all that is melody, endless goddamn song, riding that beat like a bold buckeroo bronc-buster, heroic) and the fascinating stage presence of Bon, leathery debauchee, a strange companion for the schoolkid.

Angus struggles out of his satchel and blazer, mounts up on Bon's shoulders and charges crazily into the crowd still picking out hot licks. His head is all you can see in the spotlight, jolting about, lips flaring as he gasps for breath while behind him a sound man scrabbles about trying to keep the guitar lead clear like a bridesmaid determined to be properly attentive to the most improper couple of the year...

The Marquee was a sea of sweat and people were crushed against the stage; Angus stripped down to his underwear to play while unconscious bodies were passed over the crowd. I can see Bon as clear as day, standing in the middle of it all with a huge grin plastered across his face. It took him about four years, but he'd finally conquered London.

Countdown sent a crew over to England to report on the shows and Molly Meldrum was chuffed to see a ton of people in the audience wearing school uniforms. When the episode went to air, I saw Doug Crawford interviewing AC/DC on the streets of Covent Garden and I really laughed my head off. The guys all looked silly during the interview, but Bon was the worst. He wore his favourite ball-hugging denim shorts and nothing else - at least the others managed to get their clothes on that morning. For some inexplicable reason, in the middle of the interview, Bon pulled a banana out of his pants and started to eat it.

'Oh Jesus, knock it off,' I laughed to myself.

I don't think Bon had a clue what he was doing, he was just trying to be provocative.

The Countdown producer had the whole band running around like madcap cartoon rebels, which I think was supposed to illustrate AC/DC 'on the loose' in London. It was all a bit half-arsed, though. Bon looked even worse in motion than he had standing still and it reminded me of how strange he had looked when he was playing footy. I had a flashback to when we were living with Mum in Prospect and we had Swedish neighbours up the road. Bon used to play football with their son, wearing these ridiculous little footy shorts, but he was all arms and legs; limbs shooting off in every direction. He looked like a frog shambling after the ball. (When they were done having a kick around, Bon would use the neighbours' sauna, then come bouncing back home in his little shorts with a towel flung over his shoulder. I don't know if the Swedes used their steam room naked, but Bon wouldn't have cared either way.)

When Bon first left for England I got regular letters and the odd phone call, but there was a stretch of time when he was really distant. I had my own life going on and I didn't pay much attention, I assumed he was just touring or shagging groupies. But now I think that he forgot about me because he had fallen in love with someone else. I knew that Bon had been with Silver, but I didn't know he was living with her in London. He moved into her Kensington flat when the rest of the band moved to a place in West Brompton, sometime just after Bon's birthday. I didn't know what he and Silver had between them or how he really felt about her, but I know he faded out of my life for a while. From everything I read afterwards, she seemed like the polar opposite of me; dark where I was blonde, cool where I was nervous. Silver was a junkie, whereas I barely touched drugs. She was supported by rich men in London and hung out with rock stars, and I had been the wife of a struggling musician, working two jobs to put food on the table. If there were two significant women in Bon's life, we were planets apart in every way.

With Bon on the other side of the world, so distant from my life in Melbourne, I began to feel strange that we were still married. I felt like I was living in the shadow of this increasingly famous guy and I just couldn't get away from it. I spent a lot of time around musicians, or people connected to the music industry, and most of them either knew Bon or knew of him so I was always being introduced as 'Bon Scott's wife'. It was slowly driving me mad. It's not that I minded being associated with Bon and I really cared about him a lot, but I wanted to be Irene again - just Irene, not 'Bon Scott's wife'. I made a mental note to do something about it.

One day, just an ordinary day, along with paying the gas bill and picking up my dry-cleaning, I went into the registry office and applied for a divorce.

Over in London, Silver watched Bon drink. He was up to a bottle of whiskey a day at that stage, in this endless cycle of gigs and partying. AC/DC had built up a huge head of steam in England and doors were opening for them everywhere, although Reading Festival was a big bump in the road. They played the festival at the end of August, in the rain, to a crowd of 50,000 largely disinterested people. George Young, who had flown to England to work with the guys on a new EP, was furious. Reading should have been AC/DC's launch pad to the big time, but the gig fell flat. Melody Maker called them untalented jerks, and even John Peel struggled to give them a positive review.

There were other things on the horizon, however. The revised High Voltage album had been released over in Germany and sold 16,000 copies in its first week. The band went over there in September and played a series of headline shows that brought their German fans screaming to their feet. Immediately afterwards, they joined Deep Purple's Ritchie Blackmore on a 19-date European tour, supporting his new band Rainbow. Then, a week after they returned to London, AC/DC set out on their first headlining tour of the UK; seventeen dates of muck-stirring mayhem. News of it trickled down to us through the Australian music press - wild and fantastic. Oxford Polytechnic cancelled their show because of AC/DC's 'blatantly vulgar' lyrics; in Birmingham, Angus was accused of masturbating on stage; in Liverpool, they threatened to arrest him if he flashed his arse. When the band made its triumphant return to Glasgow, they found the riot squad stationed outside the venue and piles of security inside. Bon's bagpipes were destroyed during the gig by his rabid, rioting fans.

All of this was great news for the band's reputation. By the time they returned to the capital to play their final show (to two-thousand people at the Hammersmith Odeon) they were cult heroes, at the top of their game. NME called it 'the day AC/DC conquered London':

> *...this schoolboy brat up on the rostrum smirks maliciously as his opening power chord painfully rattles through our bones and makes the unnecessary triumphant gesture of wildly tossing his cap on the floor as if to say: This is our day.*

I had just one memorable conversation with Bon in the middle of all of this. Out of the blue, he called me from England and said he was sending me a waterbed.

'A waterbed?' I repeated. I thought I'd misheard him.

'They're great,' he told me. 'You're gonna love it.'

I could not for the life of me figure out what he was thinking. I didn't know if he meant that he had a waterbed that he wasn't using anymore, or that he was so impressed with waterbeds generally that he'd decided to buy one for me as a present (did he go out *shopping* for it?!). Either way, the idea of shipping something so huge and awkward over from the UK seemed totally ridiculous.

'But I don't want a waterbed!' I told him.

'Nah, you do,' Bon laughed.

'I really don't,' I said.

And that was the end of the conversation. A few weeks later, I pulled the customs notice out of the letterbox with a sigh. *Oh for Christ's sake*, I thought. We had a few friends around that night and I was moaning about having to go and collect the thing when a guy called Nathan pricked up his ears.

'I'll take it,' he said.

I gave him the customs slip and that was the end of it. If you want to know what happened to Bon's English waterbed, you'd have to ask Nathan.

AC/DC released their third record in late September 1976, though I was a bit slow off the mark about buying it. 'Dirty Deeds Done Dirt Cheap' was the title track, which came out as a single around the same time. It was a real balls-to-the-wall rock 'n' roll song; a snarling, spitting tune with this crazy electric guitar solo. I thought it was amazing, but I wasn't desperate to have it on high rotation in my lounge room. I felt the same way about the song 'Big Balls', which was absolutely hilarious. Trust Bon to find a way to write a whole song about testicles. *Barry McKenzie would be very proud*, I thought. But again, 'Big Balls' wasn't something I needed to hear over and over again. I bought Dirty Deeds because I wanted to check in and see what Bon was up to, not because I was a slavering AC/DC fan.

There were a couple of songs that caught my attention, because they both had lines torn out of Bon's letters. 'Ride On' was about endless nights on the road; empty bottles, empty beds and regret. Something about it really got me down. It echoed that letter he wrote, *what a cunt of a night*, when he told me he was lonely. I wasn't sad because I thought he was tortured or having a terrible time out there with the band, but because he had taken the feeling he'd had that night and turned it into a song. I could almost see him, finishing his letter to me and picking up his notebook to jot down some lyrics. It was almost like he took all those feelings and just put them in a box. It wasn't something between him and me anymore, it was something he had packaged up and shoved out into the world. I guess that's what artists do, but it made me feel really sorry for him for some reason.

When I think of it now, the thing that strikes me about 'Ride On' is how early in his career Bon started to feel unhappy. As time went on, I saw and heard enough to know that he really struggled with the life he had chosen. But that life had barely even started when he wrote that song.

He hadn't hit the top yet; he was still climbing. Why was he having these miserable thoughts when everything was going so well? Why was he drinking every day and writing himself off? He wasn't like that before. Bon told RAM that 'Ride On' was about a guy who gets stuffed around by women and can't find what he is looking for, but it didn't sound like women were the problem. It was the job. Being a rock star wasn't all sunshine and roses - some part of it made him miserable.

The other track on Dirty Deeds that rang a bell was 'Ain't No Fun (Waiting 'Round to Be a Millionaire)'. The title was lifted straight out of a letter Bon wrote to me in 1975. My first reaction was to smile. I didn't know if Bon was a millionaire, but I knew he had enough money to ship a waterbed to Australia, so things had to be looking up. The song was a bit of a caricature anyway - Bon would rather die than put a patch on his jeans, and his boots were always in good nick. It was a joke, another riff on 'It's a Long Way to the Top', except for one verse. There was a verse in the song about a woman who works nine to five to support a guy who spends his time playing music and drinking beer with his mates. A woman, Bon muttered, who knew her place. I'm sure that last part was supposed to be funny, but I sure as hell wasn't laughing.

CHAPTER 10

AC/DC flew back to Australia at the end of November 1976 and held a press conference at Sydney International Airport. Outside of the conference room, there was a pack of female fans doing the whole Beatlemania bit, waiting to rub up against the newly minted rock stars. Inside the room, the guys did their best to make another bad impression. It was the return of the conquering heroes, except in this case the heroes were a pack of snot-nosed rockers giving the figurative finger to the Australian media. Bon held court and the rest of the band ploughed through cans of Australia's finest brew. At the end of the conference, Angus flashed his arse. It was the first sign of rain in a media shitstorm.

Overnight, it seemed, AC/DC became the target of a lot of bad press. There was a new trend in Sydney where teenage girls were getting tattooed with the name of their favourite AC/DC member, and the Minister for Youth got up in state parliament to wag his finger at the band and vow to stop underage tattooing. Kids started calling the phone number Bon sang in 'Dirty Deeds...' (which wasn't a phone number, but the measurements of a supposedly perfect female - 36, 24, 36) and some poor old lady was bombarded with prank calls. 'Pop Hit Makes Widow's Phone Run Hot' read a headline in The Truth. After they landed in Sydney, Bon and Angus went into 2JJ radio and Angus dropped his pants on air. Meanwhile, Sydney's 2SM vowed to stop playing their music until Angus stopped exposing himself - and that wasn't about to happen. They made as many waves as possible to promote their upcoming tour.

The guys came to Melbourne on November 30 to play a warm-up show at the Tiger Room. It was one of my favourite haunts, a music venue that was part of the Royal Oak Hotel in Richmond. It was small but it held a decent crowd - a few hundred people, squashed elbow to elbow. There was a bar along the left wall, a big stage down the back, and a great big sticky carpet in the middle. You had to fight your way to the bar and fight your way to the toilet, and good luck getting to the band room at the back of the stage. If you were into music it was a pretty popular place, but it was a broom cupboard compared to the places AC/DC could play. They were way too big for the local club scene by then.

The show was supposed to be a secret. The band didn't do any promotion and their name wasn't on the bill - it was supposed to be a small gig for the guys and their friends - but word got out and the Tiger Room was smothered in people. As far as I could tell, Angus kept his pants on. The audience was jammed up against the stage and there was no parting of the crowd to let him loose, and no one climbed the speakers or hung from the lights. It was a straight up rock 'n' roll show. But I heard a lot more than I could see, to be honest. I couldn't get anywhere near the stage and I spent the whole set peeking round people's heads, trying to catch a glimpse of Bon. It was incredibly loud and incredibly tight. There was a lot of cheering and many ferocious heads bobbing up and down, everyone having a ball.

I didn't catch up with Bon before the show, but he invited me to the after-party. Mary and I left the Tiger Room together and made our way to the Southern Cross, a plush old hotel in the middle of the city (I think The Beatles stayed there when they came through town). Bon was in one of the hotel suites and it seemed as though half the Tiger Room had gone there after the show; it was absolutely rammed with guests. I didn't recognise any of them, just a face or two from the local music scene, but they all seemed to know Bon. He was surrounded. He broke away long enough to make sure we had drinks, but we hardly had a chance to talk. He got drawn into another conversation and Mary and I just stood by and listened. He was in a self-congratulatory mood and it was all preening bullshit about the band; they had picked up two gold records for Dirty Deeds... and two platinum records for T.N.T. in Australia; they had brought England to its knees and the ladies loved them. Bon was cocky as hell and the centre of everyone's attention, basking in the spotlight. Even people who were involved in other conversations seemed to be half listening to Bon, like they were all just waiting for their turn to speak to him. I felt really uncomfortable being part of his entourage.

Not long after we arrived at the party, the room became uncomfortably crowded and someone suggested Bon clear the place out.

'Yeah right,' he said, and glanced around. He pointed at a few of his other guests. 'You go, you go and you guys go. Go on, fuck off.'

A wave of his hand and they were dismissed. It was really embarrassing for the people he fingered, but Bon obviously thought it was a bit of a joke. I was stunned. I felt anger boiling up inside of me just as my jaw was hitting the floor. I'd never seen Bon act like such a privileged rock star, surrounded by underlings and sycophants. I'd never seen anything that disgusting.

'What the fuck are you doing?' I asked him.

'If you don't like it, you can fuck off too,' he answered.

'Yep, I think I will,' I fired back.

Mary jumped in to try and make peace between the two of us, but I was totally enraged and Bon was totally full of himself. Neither of us was about to back down. I stormed out, poor Mary trailing out after me, and left him to bask in the adoration of his fans. They might be willing to put up with that behaviour, but I definitely wasn't.

AC/DC kicked off their Australian tour on December 4, with a gig at the Apollo Stadium in Adelaide. They were going to call it 'The Little Cunts Have Done It' tour, but in the end it was 'A Giant Dose of Rock 'n' Roll'. They were back in Melbourne the day after Adelaide, just in time to catch a headline in the Sunday Mirror which read 'AC/DC Boast of Sex Orgies'. The newspaper expressed a public outrage at how AC/DC were treating their daughters because the guys had bragged that they'd slept with a hundred girls in the two weeks they'd been home. I thought it was garbage at the time, but who knows. It could have been true. I was still annoyed with Bon and I wasn't interested in hearing about his rock 'n' roll antics.

The same day the orgy story broke, the band played a gig at the Myer Music Bowl, to 'wild teenage girls and male aggromaniacs', according to the reviewer from RAM. Bon insisted that the crowd listening outside the fences be let in, swelling the audience to five- thousand hysterical fans. The day after the gig, Maggie came home to find Bon asleep on a hammock at the back of our house.

'Irene's not here,' Maggie told him.

'Ah fuck,' he said, climbing to his feet. 'I forgot she was going to fucking Adelaide.'

I don't know for sure, but I think he meant to apologise (or at least pretend the whole scene at the hotel hadn't happened, which was more Bon's style). But I had left early for a Christmas break back home and AC/DC were headed in the opposite direction, to continue their tour on the east coast of Australia. They went overland through Albury, Shepparton and Canberra, over to Wollongong then up north to Newcastle, before landing in Sydney on December 12. Somewhere in there, Bon managed to send me a birthday card. It was as close to 'I'm sorry' as he ever got.

FOR YOU A BIRTHDAY POEM...

PEPPER IS PEPPER

SALT IS SALT

IF YOU AIN'T GETTING ENOUGH...

IT AIN'T MY FAULT!

Dear Ween,

Writing this from Wyong in N.S.W. We're in the middle of our tour – thankfully all is well. Except this morning I discovered I'd caught a dose of the dreaded. Just had a needle bunged in me blurt so I guess it should be ok soon.

All our concerts have been successful & we're making a lot of money. It's all going in the iron tank though. Should get a nice bonus for Chrissie though. I'll be able to buy pressos for the first time in 10 years.

I wish I had the time to come and take you out for a birthday nosh up, spunk, but we're working every night between November and Xmas. But think of me while you're stuffing yourself? I'm thinkin of you.

Bon X

P.S. Don't burn your tongue when you blow out the candle huh? Have a good one 'Rene. Love ya.

I got a poem too:

A nod means yep

A shake means not

If she'd shook a bit more

I might'nt have got what I got

I turned twenty-five in December and I was miserable on my birthday; I thought I was ancient. Probably the vat of wine I drank didn't help the situation. I was actually quite happy in general at that point. I was meeting lots of people and going out all the time. Life was treating me quite well. But young people don't have a clue what it really means to be old, do they? They waste time complaining about it before they should.

Bon didn't waste a second of his time; he was out on the road wreaking havoc with the band, offending the establishment and making headlines wherever he went. In Wollongong and Canberra, the band was warned that the power would be cut if Angus bared his arse, so instead he dropped his pants behind a 'censored' sign. In Albury, the concert programme was seized by the local police because it contained a quote from Bon about how rich you had to be to fuck Britt Ekland (the gorgeous Swedish actress who was dating Rod Stewart).

In Sydney, AC/DC played to a half full Hordern Pavilion, but controversy was at a minimum and the two-thousand-strong audience was impressed - including Rory Petrie, the reviewer from RAM:

> *...Loud seems too tame a word for the volume they inflict on an audience, it's more a 'living sound' that actually penetrates the flesh and bones until movement and rhythm come involuntarily and the audience is swept into the same current... behind the insistency lies an excellent rock/blues outfit with an amazing singer out front in Bon Scott...*

The band was scheduled to play in Tamworth a couple of days after my birthday, but the gig was cancelled by the Mayor, whose teenage daughter may or may not have been in hot pursuit of my ex. A TV crew was following the band around in the hope that something outrageous would happen, and Mike Willesee flew up to Tamworth in a helicopter when they heard that AC/DC was banned from playing. Bon called me from the road to have a grumble about it, and I agreed that the whole situation was just ridiculous.

I remembered watching The Beatles and The Rolling Stones being interviewed by these stuffy old journalists, who asked them these really strange, disconnected questions, prodding at them like they were aliens or something. And you'd see a John Lennon smirk or Mick Jagger roll his eyes, and you knew that they knew the journalist just didn't *get* it. The problem that AC/DC had, particularly in Australia, was that the media had only just got their heads around The Rolling Stones. In comes this wild, snotty rock 'n' roll band that dresses up like schoolboys, or in drag, or in ball-busting denim shorts, and the old dinosaurs just can't deal with it. First it was the mop tops, then it was the hippies, then it was this crazy bunch of Scottish-Australian yobs flashing their arses on stage. *Look at these animals! Civilisation is going down the gurgler!* they cried. It was ridiculous. Bon was pissed off and I was just bemused. What AC/DC did was so obviously playful and funny, I couldn't understand what the problem was.

'Ah well,' Bon sighed. 'I guess if we're not offending 'em we're not doing it right.'

I think the tone of things really bothered him; the amount of hatred directed towards the band. Bon hated people who were staid and stuffy and false, and he did his best to rub them the wrong way, but it was always with a smile on his face. If a sixty-year-old woman said that AC/DC were garbage, Bon wouldn't be rude or aggressive, he'd tell her that his band was brilliant. He wanted people to like him. The whole media frenzy around that tour got completely out of control, and in a funny way I think it hurt his feelings. He was just trying to show people a good time.

The first half of the AC/DC tour finished on the Gold Coast (where they were supported by The Saints) and Bon went back to Sydney to spend Christmas with the Young family. They had a couple of weeks off over the new year and Bon spent a decent part of it in Adelaide. I assumed he came over to catch up with old friends. I didn't realise Silver was in Adelaide too.

Bon came round to visit me at Mum's and he had Christmas presents for everyone, as promised. I think Mum got some perfume. He gave Fay a fantastic book about Australian graffiti, which she probably still owns. I can't remember what he gave me, but I'm sure it was nice.

'Have a look at this,' he said, pulling another present out of his bag.

It was an antique, black-and-burgundy-coloured tea set, very delicate and expensive. *Oh god, that's lovely*, I thought, *has he bought it for me?* No one had ever given me a gift like that. Who would? Bon was the only one I knew who would be that generous and Bon had never had that much money before.

'It's for Silver,' he said.

He was so pleased with himself for buying it that he didn't notice me deflate like an old balloon. *Silver, of course.* Bon hadn't actually told me that he and Silver were together, but I'd heard about it at some point, from mutual friends. I was glad he was with someone, but I wished it was someone else. She seemed so cold and hard to me, although I obviously didn't know her well. Something about her just made me uncomfortable.

But Bon seemed happy. I don't know if it was Silver or the band or having a break from touring, but he was in a great mood that day. And even though I was a little disappointed - and jealous! - I really loved seeing Bon smile.

We had tea with my Mum and chatted for a while, then he asked me to walk up to the shops with him. He wanted to go to the RM Williams store and pick up some new boots. The store was just a few blocks away, but it was a lovely, bright day in the middle of summer. We wandered slowly and enjoyed the sunshine.

I wasn't prepared for the scene at the shop. We had literally just stepped through the door when a kid beside the counter said, 'You're Bon Scott!'

Bon laughed and said, 'Yeah, sometimes.'

In a matter of seconds, he was surrounded. RM Williams is quite a conservative brand now, but it became very hip in the Seventies. The shop was full of young people buying jeans and they all knew AC/DC. Word spread fast, and the kids came straight over, holding out pieces of paper for Bon to sign.

It wasn't a horde, it was a good handful of people, but it was strange to me that every one of them was interested in Bon. It's not like we were in the middle of the city; it was a little shop in the suburbs, but it was still full of AC/DC fans. As I stood there watching Bon chat with the kids, my whole view of his life suddenly shifted. Every time I'd seen him on Countdown or heard him on the radio it was just Bon, rocking hard or acting like an idiot, and just me at home listening. I never thought about all the people that were watching and listening along with me. Of course I knew AC/DC had a lot of fans, but it was one thing to understand it in theory and another thing to watch a bunch of strangers ask Bon for his autograph. It was really, really weird.

Bon loved it. There were arms and voices coming from every direction, but he just laughed and gave them friendly answers, and took it all in his stride. He was really warm and polite, but he didn't hang out there forever; he signed every piece of paper they thrust at him and then he was off, looking for a new pair of boots. I trailed after him in amazement, trying not to look impressed. Bon, to his credit, tried not to look smug.

Bon came back through Melbourne in mid-January, when AC/DC were booked to play Festival Hall. He had a night off after that show and Mary and I took him to a bar on the north side called Martinis, a great little venue that hosted excellent bands. It was popular with the whole music crowd so there were plenty of familiar faces, but I was shocked at how many people walked up to Bon to say hello. Some of them were friends, but a lot of them were total strangers who were just AC/DC fans. It reminded me of that concert in Adelaide when no one had given him a second glance, but it was the totally opposite scene. Everyone wanted something out of him, even if it was just a quick chat. Sometimes it was more. Ross Wilson wanted phone numbers for Bon's music contacts in the United States. I didn't even realise Bon had any.

We had a great night, regardless of the interruptions. I was so relieved that Bon had climbed down from whatever ivory tower he'd been in that night at the Southern Cross. I had started to think I'd lost my friend to all the bullshit surrounding the band, but he was still in there. I think it helped that he was with his close mates, just me, Mary and crazy Pat Pickett, who hadn't seen Bon since he left for England. I think it helped that Bon hadn't just played a show.

We got roaring drunk. There was a band playing, but I don't remember who it was. We were too caught up in conversation. After several hours and many glasses of wine, Pat suggested we head off to a party. A mate of Pat's had turned up and he had a car, so the five of us decided to pile in and carry on, to find this party Pat was talking about. The mood was too good to call it a night.

I don't remember what kind of car this guy drove but it was tiny; I was crammed against the driver's side window, with Bon half sitting on my lap and Mary shoved awkwardly on the other side. Pat was apologising from the front seat.

'Are you guys alright back there?' he said.

'I'm bloody squashed!' I answered, half laughing.

Out of nowhere, Pat's friend turned round in the driver's seat and belted me across the head.

'Shut the fuck up!' he said.

There was a split second when we froze in shock, unsure of what had happened. Then Bon lunged over the seat and grabbed the driver by the throat.

'Are you crazy?' Bon shouted. 'That's my fucking wife.'

The guy managed to open his door and scrambled out of his grasp, but Bon was after him like a shot, jumping out the passenger door. I'd never seen him so angry. The guy was huge, about six-foot-four, but he was still trying to steady himself when Bon started laying punches. In a flash, our driver was on the ground with his hands braced over his head.

'You hit my fucking missus.'

Punch.

'You hit my fucking missus.'

Punch.

'You hit my fucking missus.'

Punch.

You could dance to the rhythm of it. I climbed out of the car and got one solid kick in before Bon grabbed my hand to lead me away. Mary and Pat were right behind us, completely stunned. Bon had his arm round me and kept asking if I was OK.

Unbelievably, just before we made it to the corner, we heard the bloke bellowing behind us. We turned to see him running towards us with a tyre iron in his hand.

'Jesus Christ,' I gasped, but Bon turned round calmly and punched the guy squarely in the middle of his jaw. He just ducked round the tyre iron and laid him out, *smack*, then turned to put his arm around me again. We left our attacker nursing his bruises on the footpath and went back to Martinis to call a taxi.

I was really shaken up and Bon insisted on taking me home. We hopped into a cab with Mary and headed back south to Lambeth Place, where Maggie was in the middle of her own drama. She'd driven home drunk and bounced her car off a railing on the side of the road, causing a whole heap of damage in the process. She was upset, I was upset, and Bon had copped a few blows to the head. The whole bloody house was traumatised. He didn't have to ask if he could stay, he just followed me into the bedroom and collapsed, exhausted, on my bed. I lay down next to him and closed my eyes, and seconds later I was asleep.

It was strange that Bon had called me his missus. He had a girlfriend and he knew that I'd applied for a divorce; we'd been apart almost as long as we'd been together. But there was something very beautiful about the way that word had erupted out of him in the heat of the moment. His instinct was to protect me and to let that arsehole know that he had crossed a very serious line. He didn't mean it literally. He wasn't nursing some secret desire for the two of us to get back together, it was just his way of saying *this person is important to me*. I understood and I was really grateful.

Bon left early the next morning to go and join the band, and I was left with a very irritable Maggie. She was pissed off that I'd gone to bed when she was still distressed from her accident, though she didn't give much thought to what I'd been through. It was a bit of a last straw for her and me. Ever since her Kerryn had gone to the States, Maggie had been treating me like a replacement husband. She was constantly asking me to take out the bins or complaining that I didn't pay her enough attention. She was furious with me for going to bed one night and leaving her to entertain some people we had over, even though they were friends of hers and I had work the next morning. I was starting to feel really hen-pecked - it was time to move out.

Mary had just come back from a brief stint in Sydney and she was looking for a new place; we decided to move in together. We found a house in Neill Street, Carlton, just round the corner from Martinis, and not long after Bon left town, I started a new phase of my life.

CHAPTER 11

The 'Giant Dose of Rock 'n' Roll' tour took AC/DC down to Tasmania and back through country Victoria, winding up in Moe on January 17, 1977. It had been difficult for the band, with three gigs cancelled due to public complaint and patchy turn-outs at some of the venues. They'd returned triumphant from their time in the UK, but everything had derailed in Australia and the guys blamed the backward local media. All they wanted to do was get back to Europe.

Before they left the country, they went back to Sydney, back into the studio at Alberts, to record a new album. George Young and Harry Vanda were behind the desk again, with the band set up to play live in the studio and Bon screaming next to them in a vocals booth. They wanted to make a raw, energetic record that captured AC/DC's live show; big and fast and furious. According to legend, one of Angus' amps started smoking as he played the title track, 'Let There Be Rock', but George screamed at him to keep on playing, right up until it melted. They finished the whole album in just two weeks, doing ten-hour shifts each day.

The guys had something to prove with the new record, but not in Australia and not in the UK. After releasing the international version of the High Voltage album in 1976, Atlantic Records in America had cooled on AC/DC. Their singles hadn't done very well and the rumour was that Americans didn't really *get* Bon - they literally couldn't understand what he was saying. The US label rejected the Dirty Deeds... album and they were on the verge of dropping the band altogether, but the UK office stepped in to re-negotiate the deal; the band got less money, but they still had a US record label. It bought them a little time, but the pressure was on. The new album had to open American doors.

At the end of January, AC/DC played to five-thousand people at the Sydney Festival, an inner-city gig that featured a pissed Bon introducing one of their songs as 'Can I Sit on Your Face, Girl'. A handful of shows followed in early February, including two in Adelaide and their final Australian show in Perth. That Perth gig on February 15 was Bon's last official gig on Australian soil. He left the country the next day, and two days after that he was playing in Edinburgh. It was the first night of a 30-date UK tour and the beginning of long radio silences between Bon and me.

My divorce came through on March 7, 1977. The certificate was in the mail when I came home from work. I tore the envelope open and it slid right into my lap. *That's it*, I thought. *No more Mrs Scott.* That whole ride had come to an unremarkable stop; it was an ordinary day for me and Bon was god-knows where in England, doing god-knows what. I couldn't even call him to give him the news because he was on the road - not that I'd have bothered. I didn't think it really mattered to him.

Well that's it, I thought. I felt very flat. Divorce is unpleasant even when it isn't, even when you wanted it and you'd applied for it yourself. It's a door closing on everything that was good in a relationship, along with everything that was bad. I felt a bit sad for what we'd lost.

When Mary came home, I had cracked open a bottle of wine and put a curry on the stove.

She looked at the wine and raised her eyebrows.

'Divorce party,' I told her with a smile.

In the UK, Bon was having a different sort of party and playing to ferocious crowds. AC/DC ran into trouble with a few cancelled shows, but the tour was an undoubted success - they had a lot of fans in that part of the world. The band had beaten the Sex Pistols and Thin Lizzy in Sounds' annual poll of the best new bands and they ranked 14th on the same list in NME; they were well and truly established, with plenty of decent shows to play. AC/DC had barely come to rest in London before they headed off to do twelve dates in Europe, half of which were supporting Black Sabbath. They played like dynamite, by all accounts, but the Sabbath tour didn't end well. The bass player pulled a toy flick knife on Malcolm, Malcolm threw a punch at him and AC/DC got the arse from the tour. Then in early May, bassist Mark Evans got the arse from AC/DC. Mark and Angus didn't get along and the Youngs pulled rank and asked Michael Browning to sack him, which meant the band had to find a replacement. The new recruit was an Englishman called Cliff Williams, who was a seasoned musician a little closer to Bon's age.

The guys brought Cliff back to Australia in June to break him in. They stayed in Sydney, as far as I know; Bon didn't come to Melbourne to visit and I didn't get any letters that I remember, he just called to check in and tell me he was around. They were recording again at Alberts, though Let There Be Rock had only come out in May.

'We're just mucking around with a couple of things,' Bon told me, 'So Cliff can get used to the band.'

The demo tracks they recorded would resurface on the next album more than a year later. Meanwhile, Bon was back in Bondi, hanging out at The Lifesaver, sleeping with groupies and doing guest spots with his new favourite act, a still-underground Rose Tattoo.

AC/DC shot the video for 'Let There Be Rock' around that time, with Bon as the high priest of rock 'n' roll and the rest of the band as rock 'n' roll angels. Towards the end of the shoot, the director made him climb on to the pulpit and leap over the band, which ended badly.

'I hurt my fuckin' ankle,' he told me.

I thought he looked amazing in that clip. It was probably the first music video they did where you could really see how Bon moved, although you can see him at the end of the video, crumpling to the floor. As a tune, 'Let There Be Rock' was just brilliant, especially the guitar riff. It was one of my favourites off the new album, which I'd bought when Bon was back in the UK. It was incredible, as far as I was concerned. It had high energy, full-on guitars and Bon's classic tongue-in-cheek lyrics. I thought 'Whole Lotta Rosie' was pretty crass and obvious, like the words almost overpowered the music, but when I saw AC/DC play it live it was a highlight of the show (especially decades later, when a massive balloon Rosie blew up over the stage - they really knew how to make a spectacle). Later in the year, they released 'Dog Eat Dog' as a single, and Bon appeared in the video in a big woolly Afghan coat. He lasted about two minutes in it before he had to strip it off, bathed in sweat.

'He must have just bought it,' I told Mary. 'He obviously wants to show it off.'

I liked living with Mary. She was a great housemate, much more laid-back than Maggie. She kept the same kind of hours as me, working during the day, and we loved heading out together at night. We spent a lot of our time at Martinis and we saw a lot of music, including Cold Chisel whenever they came through town. For a little while there, Mary and I were the perfect match, but it didn't last long.

At the time that we moved in together, Mary had split from her boyfriend Peter, so it was just the two of us living in the house. Fortunately for her, but unfortunately for me, Mary and Peter got back together. He moved in with us, into our semi-detached two-bedroom cottage, and things were just a little too cosy. A few months after I arrived, I became the third wheel, so I told Mary I might look for another place. She said it wasn't a terrible idea. The house wasn't big enough for three people.

I headed south of the city again, to Peel Street in Windsor, and for the first time since I'd moved to Melbourne I was living on my own. I tried sharing with a roadie friend for a while, but he'd come and gone in a matter of weeks. I decided room-mates were too much work. Chapel Street was just around the corner, with miles of shops and bars and clubs, so I figured I'd have enough enter-tainment to keep me happy. I didn't need to live with people to be connected to the world, or so I thought.

Winter set in and it was grey and miserable, always freezing cold and pelting with rain. I didn't have a car, so it was difficult to get around; the trains were unreliable and the last service was never late enough. I changed jobs and I had a great boss, so work made me happy. But nothing else was going very well. Mary was my closest friend in Melbourne but she was on the other side of the city and it was a real pain the arse to get over there and back in the evenings. She was also very wrapped up in her relationship, so she was generally less interested in going out. I hardly saw Maggie Tolhurst those days, and Sue Lovegrove had moved back to Perth.

When I first moved to Windsor, I went out by myself all the time. I'd met enough people since I'd moved to Melbourne to be confident of running into a familiar face at pubs and gigs, but I felt awkward without close friends around me. It was always a bit of a gamble as to whether or not I had a good time, and sometimes I wondered why I even bothered to try. After a while, and especially as it got colder, I gave up on going out altogether. It was all just too hard. It felt like so many people had left town or moved on, and all the fun I'd had the year before seemed to evaporate.

For the first time in my life, I felt incredibly lonely. The whole move to Melbourne seemed pointless. *What am I doing here?* I thought. *If I'm just going to go to work and come home, sleep and go to work again, I might as well be living in Adelaide.* Why didn't I move back, what was stopping me? I couldn't shake the idea once it was in my head. Winter dragged on endlessly and the rain pounded on my kitchen window. And one day, I just decided to go home.

On the other side of the world, Bon was about to launch himself on a bunch of unsuspecting Yanks. 'Let There Be Rock' was released in America on June 15, 1977, with the full support of Atlantic Records USA. There was a change of guard at the record label and the new guys really dug AC/DC, but they still couldn't get them played on the radio. Soft rock was all the rage, like the Eagles and Fleetwood Mac, and AC/DC's lyrics were too raunchy for conservative American values. The band would have to win the country over, one live show at a time.

AC/DC's first American tour kicked off on July 27, in Texas. They supported a Canadian act called Moxy, playing to five-thousand people, and within five minutes the audience was screaming its applause. *One down, twenty-six gigs to go.* They travelled across the country from Texas to Florida, playing club shows wherever they could, supporting any band that would have them. The guys had to start from scratch and do it on a budget. They ate fast food, slept in cheap hotels, and drove gig-to-gig in a station wagon with their crew trailing behind in a twelve-foot van. It was a hard road but it was worth it.

There were pockets of hysteria, even on that first tour. They supported REO Speedwagon in Jacksonville and brought an eight-thousand-strong crowd to its feet. In Columbus, Ohio, they played to four-thousand people across two club shows. Some nights they only played to twenty people, but that was twenty new AC/DC fans at least.

From the south, they went across the Midwest, then over to New York City, the world capital of cool. The guys spotted John Lennon and Yoko walking down the street and completely freaked out, apparently. They did their debut show at the Palladium that night and then raced over to CBGB's for another set, and Angus actually walked out of the venue, taking the show on to the street with his brand-new wireless guitar. From New York, the band flew across to Los Angeles and played three consecutive nights at the Whisky on the Sunset Strip. There weren't a lot of people in the audience, but the right people were there, including Iggy Pop, Steven Tyler and Gene Simmons from KISS.

I got the odd letter from Bon, but none of them survived. It was all the same rhythm. *I'm doing well, the chicks are hot, the band is great, I miss you.* I knew he was over there having fun, but I didn't know any of the details. I assumed he was with Silver, but he wrote to Mary in August and said he hadn't seen her in months. The band was constantly on the road, he told her, listing off the gigs that would consume the rest of his year:

> …everything is better than I ever thought it could be. We're touring here till Sept 7 and then it's Europe for eighteen dates, England for twenty, America for another month or so and then Australia for a tour…

I couldn't blame him for falling out of touch. He was working unbelievably hard and his career was really pumping. I didn't hear from him, but I didn't think much of it at the time. It would have been great to talk more often, but that's just because I was feeling low. It really had nothing to do with Bon. It was pure coincidence that he was hitting his stride at the point when I was completely lost.

I went to the pub alone on my last night in Melbourne. I had packed everything to get ready for the movers the next day and it was like I'd painted myself into a corner - there was nothing in the house, just a blanket on the mattress to see me through the night, and literally nothing to do. I still had a few hours to kill and the pub on the corner seemed like the only option.

You can imagine what I looked like, nursing a glass of wine alone at the Windsor Castle and thinking about my failed adventure in Melbourne. I was happy to be going home - really excited to see Fay and Mum - but it wasn't a particularly glorious moment. I felt like one big sigh, flat as a pancake and deeply disappointed. Nothing had turned out like I'd imagined and I was starting to think it never would. I wasn't really prone to self-pity, but I pulled out whatever I could muster that night, and I assumed that people would leave me to it - incorrectly, as it turned out.

'Hi,' a voice said. 'Are you by yourself?'

The guy standing beside me had very long hair, a woolly jumper and a pair of Ugg boots on his feet. People didn't usually wear Ugg boots to the pub.

'Can I buy you a drink?' he asked.

He had a really nice smile. *Why not*, I thought. *I don't have anything better to do.* I gave him a nod.

'My name's Irene,' I told him.

'Nice to meet you Irene,' he said. 'I'm Nick.'

I spent my last hours in Melbourne getting to know someone I'd never met before, a mandolin player and music teacher whose Mum lived round the corner. He was five years younger than me but he was a very mature guy, with beautiful manners and a lovely face. All we did was talk, but he lifted my spirits. It was good to get out of my own head for a while.

I flew back to Adelaide the next day and moved back in with Mum, with a truck full of my stuff making its way across the country. I was OK I think, back on familiar ground, but I didn't realise how much the city had changed. For one thing, most of my old friends were gone. I knew a bloke up the road called Ginger, a real country boy with a great sense of humour, and he took me out to some of the old venues, the British Hotel, the Largs Pier and the old Australia Hotel. The problem was, there wasn't much going on. There were bands around, I guess, but no one of interest, and the whole scene was less exciting than it had been before.

Vince moved to Melbourne about the same time that I moved home, and without him my connection to the live music scene was lost (without Vince, a lot of Adelaide's live music scene was lost, period). Cold Chisel was long gone;

the guys had settled in Sydney, where they were busy writing the songs for their self-titled 1978 debut album. Without them, my social life was a bit thin. Bruce and Anne were still in town but busy with their family and I didn't see much of the Fraternity crew. The only old friend I had left was Andrea, who was back in Adelaide. The two of us started hanging out every now and again.

I stayed with Mum and got a job as a receptionist with the Sheaffer pen company. I had no plans to move out and no idea who I would move in with - Fay already had a place with her new boyfriend, up the road. But I was OK. I fell into a rhythm of working and heading home, and having a drink at the pub with Ginger. Life was easy. The only thing I missed about Melbourne was the live music scene. I missed seeing great bands every weekend.

In November 1977, Bon did an interview with Molly Meldrum for Countdown. He was sober and calm. All the provocative antics were packed away and he just smiled and talked, totally relaxed. I hadn't seen him look that good in a long time. It was at the point when AC/DC's schedule was just gig after gig after endless slogging gig and they were three days away from their last English show, in a little town called Great Yarmouth.

'I s'pose you've all heard of Great Yarmouth?' Bon grinned.

Molly asked Bon about AC/DC's role as one of the original punk bands and Bon dismissed the idea. Punk was a fad and it was fading out, and AC/DC was better than all of those bands. They talked about AC/DC's success in England and Bon said they had built a road following. Molly asked why they had focused on their live show.

'There's nothing else,' Bon replied.

The expressions on his face were priceless; the wry smiles off screen and the understated humour. I had the sense he was biting his tongue, that he could have tumbled off into sarcasm, but he kept it together and did his job. It was the closest thing I'd ever seen to the real Bon, if there was such a thing. I was really taken with it. He seemed so confident, like he had nothing to prove anymore. It really made me smile.

'Let There Be Rock' had come out in the UK in October and it was the first record to do any business over there - it finished up at number 75 on the chart. While he was back in Europe to promote the album, Bon spent a weekend in Paris with Silver. They visited The Rolling Stones in the studio, where they were recording 'Some Girls', and met a French punk band called Trust, who were huge fans of AC/DC.

In late November, AC/DC went back to America to start another six-week block of touring. They supported Aerosmith, Styx and Blue Oyster Cult, co-headlined with Cheap Trick and opened stadium shows for KISS. They'd worked and worked and worked, and it was finally paying off. It looked to me, when I saw him on Countdown, like Bon was starting to enjoy it. AC/DC were still leagues off their peak, but Bon's success was complete in a lot of ways. He could always make more money and have more fans, but I think he'd proved whatever he had to by then, to himself as much as anyone else.

Summer rolled in and Andrea and I went to Melbourne for the weekend. She'd met a musician when he was on tour through Adelaide and planned to catch up with him interstate. They were just friends, but Andrea really fancied him. She wasn't particularly interested in music, but she was very interested in his height.

'He's even taller than me!' she smiled.

We drove across to Melbourne together and Andrea dropped me at Mary's place, where I curled up in the spare bedroom and waited for her to come home. It was so lovely to see her; we went out to Martinis the following night to celebrate. I was surprised to see a familiar face just inside the door.

'Nick! Hello,' I said.

I glanced down at his shoes. *No Ugg boots this evening.* Nick was standing with another guy I knew called Alex, who was a huge fan of The Dingoes. He'd been a regular visitor at Maggie's place.

'Do you two know each other?' Alex asked.

'Not really,' I laughed.

'A little,' smiled Nick.

He bought me a drink and we spent the night chatting, and he struck me as a really gentle guy. He was the son of a high-school principal, very well spoken. He wasn't trying to impress me with his quick wit and he wasn't trying particularly hard to be charming, he was just pleasant. He was easy to talk to. At the end of the night, we swapped addresses and phone numbers, and Nick said he would come and visit me in Adelaide. He had a gig playing mandolin with Dutch Tilders, a blues musician, and the tour would bring him through my town in the coming weeks.

'I guess I'll see you soon,' I smiled.

I liked him. He was handsome but down to earth, and much simpler than the other guys I knew, or that's how he struck me at the time. I was really looking forward to his visit.

Nick turned up, as promised, during the Dutch Tilders tour, but it was the day he was leaving to go back to Melbourne. He didn't drive, and it had been a bit of an effort to find his way to Mum's place.

'You're here!' I said.

'Not for long, unfortunately.'

It was a hot summer day before Christmas and we decided to go to the beach before I took him to the airport. We mucked around near the water and walked along the sand, talking quietly about his music and my job and the weather. It was nothing special, but it was comfortable; a nice, calm kind of a day.

At the airport, he kissed me goodbye.

Nick was nothing like Bon. There were no thrills, no excitement, nowhere near as much fun, but he was just what I needed at the time. I was a different person to the young girl who'd walked into the registry office a whole lifetime before. I'd had a lot more life experience and I wasn't as naïve. I'd had my share of misery in London and plenty of excitement in Melbourne. I was wiser and more wary, and maybe just a little bit tired. Nick was normal. That was all I wanted.

CHAPTER 12

Nick visited me regularly in Adelaide and stayed with Fay and her boyfriend. In between visits, we had a carefully coordinated phone schedule. He went from zero to a hundred in the space of a few weeks, and he made a huge effort to build the relationship, which was perfectly fine with me. He knew I'd been married before and he knew it was Bon, but it didn't seem to interest him much. Nick was one of the few people I met during that time who didn't ask me a hundred questions about my ex. Again, that was fine with me; more than fine, in fact. It was nice to feel like I was more important than Bon - even if Nick was the only person in the world who thought so.

He was into all sorts of music, but his passion was the blues. AC/DC wasn't really on his radar (he didn't see the connection). I got a good education in the blues from Nick, and he enjoyed a couple of my rock 'n' roll records. It was nice to be close to someone who loved music as much as I did. It was exciting to learn about something new.

In April 1978, I decided to go and stay with Nick in Melbourne, just to see how things went when we were under the same roof. I went for the Easter long weekend and only packed one suitcase, but I never really left. My long weekend stretched into a relationship of over twenty-five years.

Bon was back in Australia over the summer, though I barely heard from him. His relationship with Silver was on the rocks, but she was staying with him in Sydney and I don't think visiting me was high on his list of priorities. He did drop in to see Ron Alphabet, though - our old friend who warned Bon not to join AC/DC because he thought they were a 'poofdah' band. Ron's girlfriend opened the door when Bon came knocking.

'You better come and see who's here,' she called to Ron.

Bon was standing on the porch with a bottle of Jack Daniels in his hand, gesturing ostentatiously towards the limousine parked outside. It was purely for a laugh - Bon wasn't even into cars. He still got around on a motorcycle whenever he could.

AC/DC were supposed to tour Australia in early 1978 but Cliff and the roadies were refused visas; Cliff was told that if he entered the country, he'd put another musician out of work. The rest of the band was left twiddling their thumbs in Sydney, with no recourse but to complain to the press about the shitty treatment they had received. They went back into the studio, as they always did at that time of year. From January to April, AC/DC were buried at Alberts recording the follow-up to Let There Be Rock - a big, menacing, muddy record called Powerage.

Bon left the country again in April, bound for London and another UK tour, but Silver wasn't with him. When he left Sydney, she went to Southeast Asia with another man, and I think that was the end of their relationship. I'm sure they remained close, just like Bon and I had, but the last big romance of his life was over - unless you count his love affair with rock 'n' roll.

APR XX, 1978

To:
Irene Scott

1 Wilgah Street Balaclava, Melbourne

Dear Rene,

Hi sugar…I'm writing from Birmingham. We're about halfway through the Brit tour & most of us are suffering from the flu or bubonic plague or something. It's been great so far gig wise as most have been sell outs & we've been getting good reviews for the concerts and the album. Stand to make a bit of money at long last.

Speaking of which I realized I didn't do anything for you before I left but if you can hang on for a bit longer until I get a cheque I'll cross your palms with a bit of lettuce. I know you need money pretty bad and I'm sorry I can't just pop a cheque in the mail but hang on a bit and I'll fix you up (I say that to 'em all...nudge nudge).

How's everybody doing. Still having little loves here & there. Never learn, do we? Think Graeme's got the best idea, just be a hermit junkie for half the year and a seaman for the rest.

Our album went into the British charts, first week at 26, so it looks like being a top five at least. We only have about ten gigs to go on this tour & then it's off to Germany for two TV shows & then we have three weeks off before America. Cliff & I are going to Paris for a root around. I have some friends in a band there who'll put us up for a few days. They're a punk band called Trust. They recorded a couple of our songs in French & just last week got banned from French TV fir singing suggestive lyrics so I've struck again. The song they did was 'Love at first Feel'.

Alright 'Rene I'll go for now. I hope all is well and you're not diseased or preggars. Say hello to all for me. I'll try and fix you up soon.

Cheerio

Bon X

PS. I've had my hair spiked and died black...stunning.

At first, when I read the line about 'little loves here and there', I thought Bon was talking about me. Did he know about Nick already? Bon didn't know I had moved back to Melbourne because he'd sent the letter to Mum's place and she had sent it on to me. I re-read the letter. *Oh no, he's talking about himself,* I thought with a sigh. *Things obviously aren't going well with Silver if the life of a hermit junkie looks good.*

I laughed at the thought of Bon giving me money. We'd had a brief exchange a year earlier when I was moving out by myself and I complained that I didn't have enough money to set up a whole house. Bon promised to help me out the next time he saw me, but I had moved again before that happened. He always had the best intentions with me, but nothing ever came of it. He sent me a cheque for $100 when I first landed in Melbourne and that was the only money I ever saw from him, but he obviously still felt guilty about London, and the bike accident, and everything I'd done for him when we were together.

I read later than Bon became really fussy about paying people back when they lent him money, making sure he was always square with the world. I wondered if it was a hangover from our marriage. He couldn't really get square with me and it wasn't about the money. Bon couldn't repay all the time and love I had invested in him when he was too broke to appreciate it.

Nick and I lived in a two-bedroom house in Balaclava with his housemate Alex, the same guy who'd been with him that night at Martinis. They were like a pair of old women, those two, bickering about the shopping and the cleaning roster. Alex would tell me what a slob Nick was, and Nick would tell me what a slob Alex was, and I would roll my eyes and do my best to ignore both of them. We had two kelpies and a very happy household, though Alex moved out after a year or so.

Nick worked at Allans Music in the city, I got a job in the Education Department and life ticked over peacefully. Bon called my Mum and got my phone number in Melbourne and I got the odd call from him now and then. Meanwhile, Graeme started staying with me whenever he was in town. He got on very well with Nick, especially when the two of them were on the piss.

One night we were playing darts and Nick swung the dartboard from side to side while Graeme was trying to take aim, singing, 'What do we do with a drunken sailor, what do we do with a drunken sailor...'

Nick's lucky he didn't lose an eye.

On the odd weekend, we'd head up to Mount Baw Baw, where Nick's parents had a shack, roughing it in the bushes with no toilet and no hairdryer. We'd sit around the open fire while Nick and his mates played guitar, old Lead Belly and Muddy Waters tunes. Graeme came up on his motorbike once, the same weekend that Fay had come over to visit. They hadn't seen each other in a couple of years and they seemed pretty pleased to catch up, though it wasn't like it used to be. The two of them went for a spin on Graeme's bike, but the bike went for a spin too and they came off on the gravel. They were both fine though; no limbs or hearts were broken.

Over in England, AC/DC played to rapturous crowds every night. Their Glasgow show on April 30, 1978 had sold out in a single day and they decided to capitalise on the hysteria of their Scottish fans by recording the gig and releasing it as part of a live album. The stage was four metres above the crowd, but rabid audience members formed a human pyramid in an effort to reach the band, while some other enterprising folks lit fires under the seats. For a little added spectacle, the guys played the encore in Scottish football uniforms, driving the footy-mad audience wild. Later in the tour, AC/DC returned to the Hammersmith Odeon to play to an even bigger sell-out crowd, and Angus flew out over the audience with the help of a harness.

Powerage was released in May and the single, 'Rock 'n' Roll Damnation', followed two weeks later. AC/DC finally cracked the British chart with that tune. They peaked at number 24 and did their first, mandatory appearance on Top of the Pops. Then Angus drew the short straw and was sent back home to promote the album. (He co-hosted Countdown with a set of new teeth that put Bon's porcelain choppers to shame.) At the end of June, the band grouped in America, where Powerage had just been released, and set off on a sixty-three-date tour to promote it. For the next three months, AC/DC were on the road, playing sold-out club shows and stadiums with some of the biggest bands in rock music: Aerosmith, Ted Nugent, Alice Cooper, Foreigner. They had well and truly broken in the States, with very little radio support, and they had fans from the grassroots all the way to the top of the tree.

September 1978

Dear 'Rene

   Hi there. Tis about four in the morn (Mon)…the bar's closed…the bottle of Black Jack (Daniels) is empty…we're outta dope…the TV's finished…I don't have anybody to fuck…I've dropped a quaalude…I could go on all night but I won't…

   We're two days from the finish of our U.S. summer tour…It's been fourteen weeks & of course we did a month in England before that. We have six days off before touring Europe & Eng again for a month… boring init.

   I should be back in Sydney around Nov 16th as-we-is-come-back-record. We're recording for maybe a month & hopefully January will be off,,,now I've had days off since I joined this band…but not one whole thirty one day month. I'll come and see you and the family in Adelaide…oh shit, I forget you're in fuckin Melbourne. I'll come see you anyway (Just don't die between now & then. I don't feel like going to hell yet…yuk yuk…)

   Say hello to mum and Faye Barry Cath…Sounds like a port pierrie cheerio call on the Ernie Sigley show. Say hi to them all.

Love to see you soon.

Bon X

Vince Lovegrove went to see AC/DC when they played in Atlanta in August and spent the night back at Bon's hotel room, reminiscing about the old days over a bottle of scotch. Vince wrote about the evening for an article in RAM, which came out around the same time that I received Bon's letter:

> *Very impressed, I was. Personal driver, ritzy hotel, the best lookin' groupies I'd ever set eyes on. I mean, it was the real thing. I thought, if anyone deserves it, Bon does. He's been at it for long enough... he said he'd make it and he was making it in style.*

But, as Vince went on to say, Bon didn't seem to be satisfied.

'I'm getting tired of it all,' Bon told him. 'I really am getting tired. I love it, you know that. It's only rock 'n' roll and I like it. But I want to have a base. It's just the constant pressures of touring that are fucking it. I've been on the road for thirteen years. Planes, hotels, groupies, booze, people, towns, they all scrape something from you.'

Vince could be pretty creative with the truth, but I knew he was right; Bon wasn't happy. His letter was so flat and joyless. It's funny that he wrote to me that night, when we hadn't seen each other in so long. Maybe he wrote to Silver too. Wherever he was out there in the world, he obviously needed a friend.

AC/DC performed on an American television programme called The Midnight Special in September 1978, though I didn't see the clip until years later. Ted Nugent and Steven Tyler introduced the band, who played a powerhouse version of 'Sin City' from the Powerage album. Angus looked incredible, blistering across the stage like a firecracker, but for some reason I thought Bon looked terrible. He was chewing gum and his hair was awful; he had curled bangs and a perm, both growing out awkwardly. He looked like he was really unfit too, like he was bloated or he'd put on a bit of weight. And he looked like he didn't give a fuck about the performance. I don't know if I was influenced by all the other things that I'd heard about that time - by the letter he sent or the things that

Vince said - but that clip always seemed a bit wrong to me. It gave me the creeps to see Bon that way. It was like looking at a stranger.

On paper, AC/DC were on a steady climb. With the US market opening up, their albums were starting to sell in the hundreds of thousands. They released their live album in October, If You Want Blood, You've Got It, and it pushed the band higher in the UK chart than they'd ever been before, right up to the number 13 spot. They returned to Europe to capitalise on its success, playing fifteen dates on the mainland and another seventeen across the channel, with two sold-old shows at the Hammersmith Odeon to wrap up their odyssey of touring.

Bon came back to Australia at Christmas time, but he didn't come to see me as promised. He called and spoke to me every now and then. I was really deep into my relationship with Nick and I thought less about Bon as a result. It was the reverse of his time with Silver, I guess; I was in love and the rest of the world went out of focus. I didn't think Bon was in a bad way. In fact, he seemed to rally a little when he landed in Sydney. He moved into a flat in Bondi and spent his holiday trying to get fit. He got up early and went swimming at Bondi Beach, and stayed away from the heavy drinking, or so he claimed. Maybe I was right about the shape he was in in America; maybe he knew it and tried to make a change. Maybe he just wanted his beach tan back. He was always pretty vain.

AC/DC had no plans to tour Australia again. Bon told RAM that they were too drunk, too stoned and too fucked to tour, but the truth is that their home country was no longer a priority. Australia blew its chance with the band. Instead, the guys focused on recording their next album. AC/DC were on the verge of their biggest leap forward. They had built this incredible momentum over the previous twelve months and If You Want Blood... was a document of that time, but the next album they made would be career-defining.

The guys put themselves under serious pressure, but not as much pressure as the record label applied. In January 1979, the Vice-President of Atlantic Records flew to Australia to check on the progress of AC/DC's recording sessions at Alberts. Harry Vanda and George Young were back behind the desk, but the Atlantic rep didn't think they were the right producers. Atlantic wanted a hit single for the American market and they didn't think Vanda and Young could deliver, so they brought in their own guy, a producer named Eddie Kramer, who'd had huge success making records with KISS.

In February, AC/DC flew to Miami to start recording sessions with Eddie. They had a farewell dinner at the Strata Motor Inn in Cremorne before they left, and someone invited them to play in the club room next door. Malcolm, Angus and Bon got up for an impromptu set, with George Young on bass and labelmate Ray Arnott on drums. They powered through half a dozen songs including 'Let There Be Rock'. It was the last time Bon performed in Australia.

AC/DC's time in Miami was short. Eddie Kramer expected them to turn up with polished songs, ready to record. The band were used to building things in the studio, with George testing chords on the piano and Bon scribbling lyrics out in the kitchen. Kramer said Bon was struggling with his lyrics and that his drinking was a serious problem. AC/DC thought Kramer was a bad fit who didn't understand their process. The relationship lasted a few unproductive weeks.

When Malcolm called Michael Browning to tell him they needed a new producer, Browning suggested John 'Mutt' Lange and Atlantic agreed to the change. The band had to start over, which blew out their schedule, and a series of shows they had booked in Japan in March were cancelled. Instead, they flew back to London to start over on the album with Mutt. For the next two months, they rehearsed and recorded, doing fifteen-hour days at London's Roundhouse Studios, then at Chalk Farm Studios, then at Basing Street. AC/DC clicked with Mutt and he got the best out of the piles of material they had collected. He captured the raw sound of the band, but gave their songs a perfect tune-up, and everyone was confident they got the record that they needed. The album was called Highway to Hell and it was AC/DC's breakthrough.

Bon's world was about to open up again, just as mine was busy contracting. After a year with Nick I found I didn't go out much anymore, but I was perfectly happy to stay in. I didn't want much out of life except creature comforts and a few laughs every now and then.

Nick wore old-man pyjamas with hankies stuffed in the pocket and grandpa slippers. He would never get on a motorbike, or do any hard labour, because he wouldn't want to damage his guitar hand. He had studied art at school, and English and history, and he always said his head was full of useless facts and figures. He was knowledgeable and he was patient, and I could ask him anything without being afraid that he would think less of me.

When Mary met Nick, she said, 'She must really like you because she hasn't hung shit on you yet.'

It was funny, but she was right too. I didn't feel like I had to defend myself by going on the attack. It was a safe relationship for me.

I fell pregnant in June 1979. I was twenty-eight, which seemed pretty old in those days. I figured I had plenty of life experience to share with the kid, if nothing else. I worried that we would struggle financially, but we had people looking out for us; Vince and Helen gave us a heap of baby things, including a big green cot covered in rock 'n' roll stickers.

I fell victim to every cliché in the book. I was obsessed with knowing how big my baby was, studying baby books and looking at growth charts. I went to antenatal classes and I spent a lot of time with my hands on my stomach, wondering when the baby would move. And I had all these romantic visions of a cuddly thing lying quietly in the basinet beside me (ha ha). It was such a lovely period of my life.

September, 1979

65 West 55th St New York City

Dear Irene,

Hi kid, how's tricks? At the moment I'm in California to start our "Fall" tour. We've been running round like blue arsed flies this past couple of months between America, Europe and the UK doing all kinds of concerts, TV shows and promotion shit for the new album. Have you heard it yet? I don't even know if it's been released in Aus yet. It's on the charts all over the world and selling like hot crumpet. I think we've done it with this one. Should be able to pay the rent for a couple years.

I wanna buy a house in California, a place like Fraternity had. I have some friends here who are in the house and real estate business & I've had some good offers but it'll take another year and I'm in no hurry. It's just a nice feeling to know you can do it at last.

How's life in Melb? If your still there that is. Are you still with the beau? I hope everything's working out good for you.

I might get a chance to see you arround Xmas-New Year. I plan to get to Sydney around the 23rd of Dec, buy a bike and ride to Perth. I've got a couple of weeks off & I just want to take it easy and unwind (this touring takes it out of you.) So anyway, write to me and tell me if you'll in Melb or Adelaide arround that so I'll know where to bring your presso.

I'm still a very single man and having a ball right now. America's certainly the place for a good time. I've become a bit of an alco (what's new…) But I'll cut down when I go on holiday & leave off for a couple of hours.

I've got a lot to tell you but I figure it can wait till I see you next. I'm not doing a whole lot of letter writing at the moment you might have noticed but I'm always thinking of you.

Say hi to Graham if he's still alive. Maybe he'd like to ride to Perth with me. I'll try to see you soon.

Cheerio for now

Bon X

The card I got from Bon came via his new management agency, Leber-Krebs. It had a Poersch painting on the cover, of crumpled jeans and a Hawaiian shirt. Lord knows where he picked it up; he was always on the move. The minute AC/DC were done recording their album in London, they went straight back to America for a fifty-three-date tour.

Poor old Michael Browning had gone the way of Mark Evans, dropped from AC/DC when he'd outlived his purpose. Leber-Krebs represented Aerosmith and Ted Nugent; they were the highest-profile rock management company in the world at that point, and where AC/DC were headed they needed the big guns. Sales of If You Want Blood... had hit half a million units. The new album would blow that figure out of the water.

Highway to Hell was released on July 27 in the UK and August 3 in the US, and it raced into the charts on both sides of the Atlantic. NME called it 'The Greatest Album Ever Made' and it made its way into the Top 10. It climbed to the number 17 spot in the States, a market twenty times the size of Australia. It was the explosion the band were looking for - and working for - their entire careers.

The day after the album had come out in the UK, AC/DC played in front of eighty- thousand people at the World Series of Rock at Cleveland's Lakefront Stadium. Three weeks later, they supported The Who at Wembley Stadium. Juke said their performance was perfect.

Bon had toured Europe and returned to the States by early September, when he wrote to me. The band was travelling with a crew of twenty-five, playing three or four shows a week, criss-crossing continents. I'd fallen into a bubble after I got pregnant. I wasn't reading music magazines anymore; I don't even know if I watched Countdown. Bon may as well have been describing life on Mars. He asked me if I'd heard Highway to Hell and I hadn't - in fact, I don't think I actually bought the record until several years later. I didn't care about the music industry, or even the music, I just wanted to know how my friend was travelling.

Bon sounded so different to me. He was so matter-of-fact about his life, so flat and literal, it struck me as a bit odd. As always, I was glad to hear that he was doing well. I was glad that he had money in the bank; there was no one who understood as well as me how important that was to Bon. It was funny to think of us scraping together pennies to live on cheap brandy and fried rice, and then hear Bon talk about buying a house in California. *Life is really amazing*, I thought. *You never know where you'll end up.* I just wish he sounded a little bit more excited about things.

I kept in touch with Isa Scott over the years, writing letters and letting her know what was going on in my life. I liked her; she was a good woman. As much as she adored her son, Isa could see the wrong that Bon had done to me so she didn't hold me responsible when the relationship ended. The two of us remained friends for many years.

I told Isa that I was pregnant and Isa told Bon, and he called me from somewhere in America. I was so surprised to hear from him that I forgot to ask about the tour, or the house, or the album, or anything.

'I heard you're preggars,' he said, feigning surprise.

'Yeah, I am,' I laughed. 'What about it?'

I'd told Bon about Nick, but they'd never met and he wanted to know if Nick would make a good father.

'Compared to who?' I grinned.

Towards the end of the call, Bon got really serious. He wanted to know if I was OK, and did I need any money.

'Do you need any help or anything?' he said gently.

'Nah, we'll be right,' I told him with a sigh.

Bon's financial life had changed a lot, but mine was still a bit of a struggle. I'd have to go straight back to work when the baby was born just to make ends meet and it was a disappointing place to be, not that that was Bon's fault. I didn't think I was entitled to his money, but I was annoyed by the way he offered it. *What do you reckon?* I thought to myself. *Of course I need money.* But I didn't want a hand-out. I know that Bon had good intentions, but he really wounded my pride.

I wrote to him a few days later to get it off my chest. I don't know if it was the pregnancy making me soft, but I wanted to be honest about it. I don't remember exactly what I wrote but I didn't ask him for money - which is why the response I got was so bloody confusing. He sent me a postcard from the States with a picture of old Native American warriors on one side and a strange kind of apology on the other.

I'm on a plane going to Seattle, Washington State as I write this. Thanks for the letter. I'm a cunt I know but I'll fix everything up by the end of the year 'Rene. I'll be back in January and I'll come see you. Say hi to all for me.

Miss you
Bon X

AC/DC spent the last couple of months in 1979 on a 'Highway to Hell' tour through Britain and Europe, playing fifty dates in fifty-eight days. The tour was virtually sold out before it even started, including two nights in the band's adopted home of Glasgow and five nights at the Hammersmith Odeon. In Paris, they played two shows in a single day and both sets were filmed, with the second released later as the centrepiece of a documentary, 'Let There Be Rock'. It captured AC/DC at their raw peak and Bon in the most glorious moment of his whole rock 'n' roll career. It was commented later that he didn't look his best, but I didn't see it. People were just looking for clues for what came next.

Mick Cocks of Rose Tattoo joined AC/DC on part of the UK leg, riding around on the tour bus and enjoying the party with Bon. Years later, he told a journalist that Bon was talking about me a lot during that time, saying there were things that he wanted to sort out. I didn't know what to make of it. I guess it's possible that Bon had pushed everything aside until he made it to the top. And maybe when he got there, he had time to stop and think. I don't know because we had never really talked about. And unfortunately, we never got the chance.

CHAPTER 13

Nick and I came home on New Year's Day to find a box of booze on our doorstep.

'That'll be Bon,' I said. 'He'll be back.'

Bon wouldn't have left the alcohol behind unless he was planning to come back and drink it.

AC/DC had played the last date of their UK tour a few days before Christmas and Bon jumped straight on a plane to Australia. He'd been going non-stop almost nine months and everyone who was around him during that time said his drinking was completely out of control. If he wasn't pissed he was sleeping it off, preparing to get pissed again the minute he woke up. People were worried about him, even in that bizarre rock 'n' roll world. Even in the midst of an endless party, Bon's behaviour didn't look right.

I don't know if it was the relief of coming home, but he seemed fine when I saw him. There were no demons perched on his shoulder; he wasn't haggard or gaunt. He looked pretty great, actually, just the same old Bon. I was the one who had changed.

Bon took a step back when I opened the front door, eyes wide.

'Jesus Christ,' he said. 'Look at the size of you.'

I was nine months pregnant with a belly to show for it.

'Give it a rest,' I laughed.

He came in to give me a hug, then leaned back and prodded my stomach with his finger.

'Just checkin' it's real,' he grinned.

I was so happy to see him. It had been a couple of years; way too long. I missed that big smile on his face.

'Are you alright?' he asked me.

'Yeah I'm good,' I replied. 'Come in, I'll introduce you to Nick.'

Nick and Bon were pretty different characters but they were both good at putting other people at ease. I wasn't worried about the two of them; I knew they'd like each other. Bon reached up to shake Nick's hand and Nick reached down to shake his, and the next thing I knew they were deep in conversation and I was getting them beers.

The guys spent the day drinking and talking about music while I sat quietly and listened. Bon had been to a gig on New Year's Eve and he said it was a pretty wild night. Nick was in a little throw-together rock band and Bon said he'd like to see them while he was in town. He said he'd missed a lot of new music while AC/DC were on tour because he had no time to buy records and nowhere to play them, so Nick started pulling out vinyl and playing him bits and pieces of songs. Bon loved Eric Clapton's Slowhand album and some of the old blues records that Nick played. Nick told him how much he liked 'Girls Got Rhythm' from Highway to Hell, and Bon agreed it was a fantastic song. Bon told Nick that AC/DC had recorded 'Gloria' as a B-side for 'Jailbreak' but it never got released.

Out of nowhere, Bon told me he'd read this really great book.

'It's called 'The World According to Garp,' he said. 'I've been meaning to get it for ya.'

I told him I'd look for it the next time I was in town.

Later Bon said something funny and I erupted with a big, deep laugh, straight from the belly.

Bon looked at me with his eyebrows raised and said, 'Jesus Christ, was that from the kid?'

He talked a lot about AC/DC, but most of it sailed over my head. *Here we go*, I thought, *ho hum*. Nick was really interested but I drifted off, wondering when Bon would have time to buy that house in California. The band was due back on tour at the end of the month and they were already planning their next album. It was no wonder he talked so much about AC/DC - there wasn't much else in his life.

As the afternoon wore on, Mary and her boyfriend Peter came round. Nick fired up the barbecue and they joined us for dinner, drinking and laughing as the evening rolled in.

'I'm out of scotch, 'Rene, will you take me to the bottle shop?' Bon asked.

I was the only one sober enough to drive, so we climbed into the car and whipped up the street; it was the last time I was ever alone with him. Bon poked fun at my huge, pregnant stomach and we laughed all the way to the shops. I can see him like it was yesterday; hair long and fluffy, wearing an orange Hawaiian shirt, grinning at me from the passenger seat while the traffic rolled past his window. He seemed happy.

Bon stayed at our place that night, in the spare bed beside the cot that Vince had given us. I was so excited about the baby that I'd filled the cot with baby crap; clothes, sheets, wraps and soft toys. My rock 'n' roll ex-husband crashed out drunk next to a pile of nappies and bunny rugs.

The next day, Mary came round to pick Bon up. I wasn't up for too much fun at that stage, so Bon went to stay with Mary and Peter, but we made plans to go out to dinner than night. Bon wanted to take us all to a Japanese restaurant.

He called me that afternoon to make sure I was coming but I was just too knackered. There would be too many people there and too much action. I was still exhausted from the night before. I told him I'd catch up with him the next day.

'Alright,' Bon replied. 'Still love ya, 'Rene.'

It was lovely, the way he said it; it just rolled off his tongue. I wanted to respond but I hesitated. What was I going to say, with my boyfriend sitting in the other room? *Love you too, Bon*, I thought.

Bon never made it to the restaurant that night. He started boozing at the Station Hotel near Mary's place and the evening turned into another long party. Mary had a gorgeous girlfriend called Margaret who joined them for a drink, and she and Bon ended up going home together. He stayed at her place for a couple of nights and I invited them both round for dinner.

When they arrived I looked at them in mock horror and said, 'My husband! My best friend! How could you!'

Poor Margaret just looked confused.

Bon wanted to go out after we ate and Nick suggested he check out Sam See's new band.

'You coming?' Bon asked me, but I shook my head.

'I'm too tired,' I told him. 'I'm sorry.'

Later that night, Nick and I were lying in bed reading.

We heard a car pull up out the front and the doorbell rang, and Nick got up to answer it. I could hear Bon's voice in the hallway, asking if I was around.

'She's asleep,' Nick said. 'I'm sorry mate.'

I was awake, but I couldn't be bothered getting up. *I'll see him tomorrow*, I thought. I listened as Nick closed the door and Bon drove away in a taxi.

I wish I could have that moment back; I would have done it differently. I'd have gotten out of bed and walked to the front door, put my arms around Bon and said goodbye.

For me, being married to Bon Scott was a mixed blessing. When you marry someone who becomes a superstar, people tend to remember just that one thing about you. Your life is reduced down to one little detail, like a caricature. I was a whole person before Bon came along and I have had a whole complicated existence since he died, but sometimes it feels like our marriage is the only thing about me worth mentioning. It's not a happy thought. I have avoided telling workmates and new friends about Bon in the past because I wanted them to get to know me, just Irene, before they started thinking of me as 'Bon Scott's wife'. I've lived most of my life in his shadow and it's tiring, sometimes.

But I wouldn't trade my time with Bon for anything. He was one of a kind. He was a larrikin, but he was no idiot. He liked to be liked, but he didn't try to impress people; they responded to him because he was genuine and funny, generous and kind. He was the life of the party with a poetic soul, and once he started loving you he never stopped. It really was a privilege to know him.

Bon and I understood each other and we made each other laugh. We had an incredibly strong connection. Maybe if things were different we could have had more time together, but things were what they were. I don't regret it, I shared him with a lot of people, and they all loved him as much as I did, but I treasure the little piece of him that was mine.

Dear Bon,

Love you too.

We had a very short and very bumpy ride together. I am so sorry you didn't get to see the end results of your amazing journey. I'm sorry you weren't able to enjoy your incredible success. You deserved it, all of it, and more.

I will always miss you.

Irene x

ACKNOWLEDGEMENTS

A huge thank you to my amazing co-writer, Simone Ubaldi. She worked tirelessly and had a very hard task, but I am very proud of what we have achieved together.

Thank you to Ingrid Ohlsson and Pan Macmillan Australia for their interest, support and publishing of the book My Bon Scott in Australia and New Zealand and to James Young for helping to get the story out there.

Thank you Mark Neeter, Red Planet Zone for publishing the book for a wider audience of Bon Scott fans.

Thanks also to Jim Slade for your perseverance to have this book published for fans everywhere.

The memories contained in this book are old and rusty, and it took a bit of help to get the wheels turning again. I wish to thank my sister Fay and my friends Vicki and Mary for their help with this process.

HAVE A DRINK ON ME

ROCK ATLAS
UK AND IRELAND SECOND EDITION

800 great music locations and the
fascinating stories behind them

Rock Atlas is more than just a guide to over 800 music locations. You can visit many of the places or simply enjoy reading this extraordinary fact-packed book's fascinating stories. Some are iconic, others are just plain weird or unusual, such as Bob Dylan turning up unannounced on a public tour of John Lennon's childhood home or the musical park bench commemorating Ian Dury's life that plays recordings of his hits and his appearance on Desert Island Discs.

Providing insights into many performers' lives, Rock Atlas includes artists as diverse as The Beatles, Sex Pistols, Lady Gaga and Lonnie Donegan. Presented in an easy-to-read, region-by-region format, every entry provides detailed instructions on how to find each location together with extensive lists of the pop and rock stars born in each county.

Illustrated with hundreds of rare, unseen and iconic colour and black and white photographs, Rock Atlas is a must for anyone with an emotional tie to contemporary music and the important places associated with it.

On sale now

For information on Red Planet books visit www.redplanetzone.com

Heddon Street, London **David Bowie** poses for the iconic **Ziggy Stardust** album cover

ROCK ATLAS

800 great music locations and the fascinating stories behind them

Written and researched by David Roberts

PLACES TO VISIT

Album cover & music video locations **Statues, graves memorials & plaques** Venues, festivals and places that influenced songs

Hundreds of new photos and facts

ROCK ATLAS USA
THE MUSICAL LANDSCAPE OF AMERICA

ROCK ATLAS is more than just a guide to 650 music locations across the USA. You can visit many of the places by following the book's detailed instructions or simply just enjoy reading the fascinating, fact-packed stories behind each entry.

Seek out the quirky record stores, find the iconic recording studios, make a pilgrimage to memorials and statues, check out the best festivals, and visit the exact spot where your favorite album cover was photographed. Rock Atlas USA will be your guide.

Providing a unique insight into musicians' lives and songs through the places linked to them, Rock Atlas USA includes stories featuring artists as diverse as The Beatles, Lady Gaga, Muddy Waters, Bruce Springsteen, Kings of Leon, and Otis Redding.

Illustrated with hundreds of rare, unseen, and iconic color and black and white photographs, Rock Atlas USA is a must for anyone with an emotional tie to contemporary music and the important places associated with it.

On sale now! To find out more visit:
www.redplanetzone.com

650 GREET MUSIC LOCATIONS

The musical landscape of America

Album cover & music video locations

enues, festivals, udios, & homes

tatues, graves, museums, memorials, & plaques

ROCK ATLAS USA

David Roberts

Exclusive interviews and more than 500 fascinating photographs

Crosby, Stills & Nash
Cover shoot by Henry Diltz, West Hollywood, 1969

LUS!

E BRILL BUILDING • DEAD MAN'S CURVE • THE JOSHUA TREE • PAISLEY PARK • AND MORE

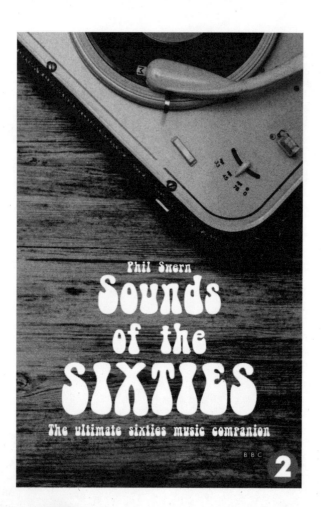

Phil Swern

Sounds
of the
SIXTIES

The ultimate sixties music companion

BBC
2

BBC
RADIO **2**

SOUNDS OF THE SIXTIES

This book contains fascinating facts about memorable hi
key Sixties artists, including details of hard-to-fin
alongside many hidden gems that are rarely heard sin
initial Sixties release. Plus there are hundreds of enthrall
stories and behind-the-scenes info from producer F
Collector' Swern. This is a comprehensive collection tha
that music fans and hardened Sixties collectors will

FROM JAMES TO JIMI
How 15 months in England made Hendrix a star

JIMI HENDRIX
MADE IN ENGLAND

This book uncovers his life in London and explains how James became Jimi. Featuring new interviews with friends, musicians and colleagues, *Hendrix: Made in England*, contains masses of new insights and provides a fascinating picture of that time. It records a remarkable period as pop started to give way to rock and Hendrix straddled both with hit singles and top-selling albums.

THE TRIP IS THE STORY OF A BUNCH OF MUSICAL DESPERADOS FIGHTING THE BUSINESS, FIGHTING AUDIENCE INDIFFERENCE AND FIGHTING MUSICAL PREJUDICE AS THEY PLAYED A NEW KIND OF COUNTRY. IAN DUNLOP AND HIS FRIEND AND FELLOW INTERNATIONAL SUBMARINE BAND MEMBER GRAM PARSONS TRAVELLED ACROSS AMERICA, PLAYING AGAINST A BACKDROP OF HOLLYWOOD HOPEFULNESS, THE VIETNAM DRAFT DODGE AND THE BANDS DOGGED INSISTENCE THAT UNFASHIONABLE COUNTRY MUSIC COULD BE ANY KIND OF CREATIVE FORCE IN THE ROCK ERA. THIS IS A ROAD TRIP IN THE GREAT AMERICAN TRADITION AND THE EVENTS OF THE MID-SIXTIES CRACKLE OFF THE PAGE.

THE ULTIMATE ROAD TRIP ACROSS LATE SIXTIES AMERICA

THE TRIP

IAN DUNLOP

IAN DUNLOP

THE TRIP

"IT ENDED TOO SOON FOR ME, I WANTED MORE"
DAVE GRIFFIN, 'THE GRAM PARSONS'

"...STRAIGHT FROM THE HEART."
BILLY RAY HERRIN, 'HICKORY WIND MUSIC'

"THIS ISN'T A BOOK, IT'S A JOURNEY, A TRIP THROUGH THE '60'S WE ALL EITHER DREAMED ABOUT, LIED ABOUT OR ACTUALLY TOOK."
PETE GALLAGHER, WMNF RADIO

AVAILABLE SOON AT WWW.REDPLANETZONE.COM

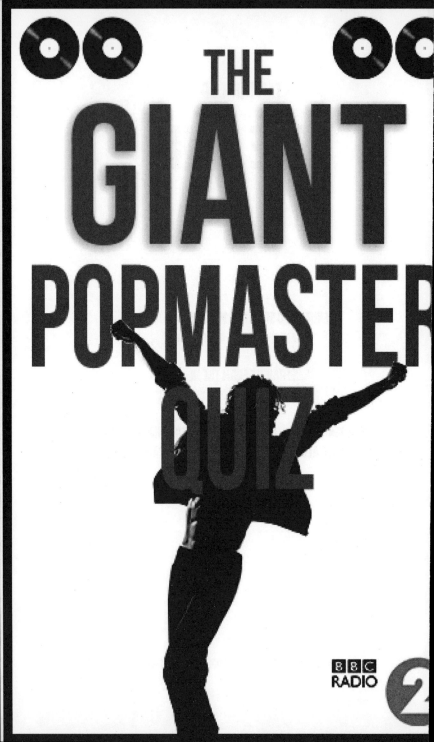

RADIO 2'S POPMASTER QUIZ HAS BEEN THRILLING LISTENERS TO THE KEN BRUCE SHOW FOR 20 YEARS. NOW YOU CAN ENJOY THE POP QUIZ IN YOUR OWN TIME AT HOME, IN THE PUB, OR AT A PARTY WITH YOUR FAMILY AND FRIENDS. THIS NEW GIANT QUIZ-BOOK IS PACKED WITH OVER 3800 QUESTIONS TO KEEP YOU ENTERTAINED, AMUSED, AND INFORMED FOR HOURS. WRITTEN BY POPMASTER'S EXPERT QUIZ-SETTERS PHIL SWERN AND NEIL MYNERS, THIS BOOK IS A MUST FOR POP TRIVIA FANS, MUSIC LOVERS AND QUIZ ADDICTS ALIKE!

AVAILABLE NOW AT WWW.REDPLANETZONE.COM

77
SULPHATE
STRIP

AN EYEWITNESS ACCOUNT OF THE YEAR THAT CHANGED EVERYTHING

FEATURING:
SEX PISTOLS
THE STRANGLERS
THE CLASH
THE DAMNED
THE RAMONES
THE VIBRATORS
THE TUBES
THE JAM
BLONDIE
X-RAY SPEX
SHAM 69

"

THE BOYS
THE DRONES TELEVISION
GENERATION X
THE HEARTBREAKERS
ALTERNATIVE TV
IAN DURY
RADIATORS FROM SPACE
AND MANY MORE

BARRY CAIN

The acknowledged seminal work on punk: a fast-paced trip through an extraordinary year. This book includes major new interviews with Paul Weller, Johnny Rotten, Strangler Hugh Cornwell and Rat Scabies of The Damned.

www.redplanetzone.com